LIVING LIFE GODDESS POWERED

The Everyday Goddess Revolution

Published by: The Everyday Goddess Revolution

Edited by: Penny Thresher, Corner House Words

Copyright 2021 The Everyday Goddess Revolution

www.theeverydaygoddessrevolution.com

ISBN: 9798705275724

Access over $2000 worth of free coaching, workshops and resources that accompany this book here:
http://bit.ly/joingoddessacademy

"In her chapter "Goddess, Who me?", Coach Judy does an amazing job helping us women recognize the misinformation constantly fed to us by others and in our own heads...and then gives such great direction on what to do about it! Being my own worse enemy on a regular basis, I found her tips so relevant and incredibly helpful! There is great wisdom here."
-Lori Osborn, Biz Bolster Solutions, Web design for business and non- profits

"Yes yes yes yes.........Totally and utterly everything I've ever felt about my soul was in Yolandi's chapter, suddenly my life with my soul and my journey made sense. Through reading of your healing and journey, I understood my own. Thank you so very much."
- Elle, Serendipity, Mind Body Soul

"Jena Robinson is the voice you didn't know you've been looking for. Her narrative chronicling her journey from a voiceless child to an empowered goddess goes beyond the scope of a short biography and into an exploration of how we can all overcome the challenges holding us back. Covering an extensive amount of ground in a short sum of words, her piece describes points of conflict in her life, illuminates how she identified emotional patterns, tracks her discovery and implementation of eclectic healing approaches, and offers pointed empowerment advice for the audience. The narrative transcends her singular story and resonates with all women who will see themselves in her words. There is a deeply personal and magnificently inspiring feel in the way she captures her journey of realizing her ability to change her reality and help those around her do the same. Her language is ethereal, encouraging, and filled with the love, empathy, and positivity that she radiates as a fully actualized goddess. Jena Robinson's intimate, engaging, and inspiring narrative has many lessons to be discovered in it; I encourage everyone to read it. "
-Brittany Petrilli, Artist & Teacher

"Randi's chapter was moving, beautifully written and expressive. Reading her story made me realize behaviors to be aware of and that we can always heal from negative experiences. Sharing our journey with others allows us to be the light for other women. Thank you Randi for being courageous."
-Jenn Reinke, Strategic Business Coach

CONTENTS

INTRODUCTION

Welcome Goddess,

I cannot put into words how exciting it is that you found this book and that you are about to read the wisdom of some incredible spiritual leaders from around the world, and then embark on a journey living a life Goddess powered.

My heart is wide open with love and joy that you will be touched by the words in this book and begin your own journey of exploration and reconnection.

The vision for this project came to me during a meditation, and the moment I decided that, yes, yes, I would bring this vision to life, EVERYTHING flowed into place. It was a Divine experience and I know that you discovering this book is an extension of that Divine intention. The intention that has flowed through from the moment we all came together and began to write.

In my vision I could see the significant power that exudes from a woman the moment she remembers who she is.

That inner knowing, hearing the whispers of her soul.

When sleeping women wake, mountains move.

You are the Goddess rising.

You are awakening to your truth, pure potential and unravelling the stories that you placed upon yourself in your sleeping state.

You are shining a light from within, embracing all of who you are.

You know the power you hold, and you are ready to create a life on your terms, aligned with your heart.

You see yourself in all other women.

You see the perfection of all of life's experiences thus far, knowing they brought you to this very moment.

You are a woman who is standing in her power and saying – THIS IS ME.

It is time to recognise the everyday Goddess within. The chapters that follow are filled with wisdom that will become the starting point of your journey back to the truth of who you are.

I see you. I believe in you. I cheer you. I love you.

Now is the time to live your life Goddesspowered.

Leanne x

Founder – The Everyday Goddess Revolution
www.theeverydaygoddessrevolution.com

PS - Remember to access all the free coaching, workshops and resources that support this book and your journey into living life goddess powered!

http://bit.ly/joingoddessacademy

You are in a partnership with your soul.

"Our deepest fear is not that we are inadequate," Marianne Williamson writes in A RETURN TO LOVE. "Our deepest fear is that we are powerful beyond measure. It is our light, not our darkness, that most frightens us. "

I love this quote, BUT I have always thought that our greatest light lies in our darkness. Those parts of you that you were forced to suppress, those parts of you that you were not allowed to show. Maybe your parents made you hide it, or society, or you yourself. We all carry a part of us that is hidden within and in there are your gifts. Have you ever looked at your shadows? Looked at the parts of you that scare you, or make you feel uncomfortable?

Let me tell you my story. Maybe it will give you some insight into my reasoning. Ever since I can remember I have been outspoken. Not loud, but rather opinionated and a little "out there" with my words. I loved drama club and never missed an opportunity to be on stage. Then one day, during my last year in High School, something awful happened.

We had to do a book review in English class. I am an Afrikaans South African and English is my second language, but I loved reading and had just finished an amazing book about Morgan La Fey and some awesome witchy stuff. Very keen, and excited, to share this brand-new world I had uncovered with my classmates, I stood up and suddenly, I drew a total blank. I could not remember anything. I stood there, watching everyone staring at me, hearing the giggles in the back of the class, and watching my teacher trying to decipher my ramblings. It was terrible. A situation that literally broke my self-confidence. I was gutted. And from that moment, the struggle with sharing my voice began.

After leaving school I found myself resisting standing up and leading. I was very confident when there were only a few people around me. I could speak my mind and share my words, but the moment I had to stand up in front of a crowd, I totally freaked out. I felt sick, with clammy hands, a racing heart and major anxiety. Reluctantly I did this a few times, but it was extremely overwhelming and lead to a few major panic attacks which made me run and hide each time. The fear of judgement within me was so strong and overwhelming.

In my mid 30s I left my corporate life as a Business Analyst to pursue a new-fangled career on the woo-woo side of life.

I had studied reading the Akashic Records. If you are not familiar with this concept, allow me to quickly explain. This is basically an energetic database of all our past lives, and we are able to access these and discover information that can help us heal those parts of us that we have hidden away. Needless to say, I wanted to explore where in my previous lives I lost my voice.

I found a few lives where my old witch wounds surfaced, being hung, and burnt at the stake came through quite strongly. These old wounds wanted to be healed in this lifetime and showed up on that seemingly innocent day in my English class.

Even the smallest and most random events in our current lives can open up our past life wounding. These need to be looked at and healed.

I spent the next few years learning to understand my fear and focusing on my voice. I knew that the only way I could step back into my power and uncover that hidden part of me was to face it head on. So, I made a promise to myself to do as much as I could to overcome this intense fear.

 I held my first workshop, teaching people about the Akashic Records and reading for them. Again, felt like I wanted to die. I was so scared, but I masked it well and cracking jokes and keeping things light saved me. The next workshop was arranged, and it got a little easier, but the fear was still there. I kept on working on it and delving deeper. Discovering more information about my fear of judgement and how I was not actually fully living my truth. There was more to heal.

Next came the opportunity to lead meditation gatherings. This was so intense, but again I kept going, knowing that somehow, I could heal my voice obstacle. I kept going. Then I started recording videos for my own YouTube channel. I knew deep inside that if I just pushed through, I could get my body to start relaxing and get out of the fight or flight mode every time. The great thing was that the more I did these group meditations and YouTube videos, the more comfortable I felt. A bit like riding a bike. I kept practicing and then it all felt easier and easier.

But fear of judgement was still a huge obstacle for me, and I needed to understand and dissect it more (my inner business analyst wanting to understand the issue). I really took time to understand my truth.

For many years I had been listening to everyone around me, trying to mould myself to their ideas and opinions because I did not trust myself. I did not know how to listen to my own inner guidance.

I took time and sat with my beliefs, I took them apart and reassembled them, to start showing my own unique truth. Accepting that I was weird and off the wall with my ideas was a big step. Things like past lives and being a Star seed was not something looked kindly upon by society, especially not with my strict Christian upbringing. But deep inside I knew these things were part of my truth and by understanding it more I would be able to move closer to who I am.

The next challenge was to go live on Facebook. A bigger platform with people watching and commenting while I spoke and shared my ideas, my opinions, and the most vulnerable parts of myself. It had to be done, but I chickened out many times, the fear still intense and overwhelming. It was frustrating, as I had done so much healing work, and it felt as though this was a battle that I was never going to win.

Then one day, while at a business retreat, it finally dawned on me – my Soul and I needed to start working together. I was still allowing myself to be led by others, still not properly listening to my inner guidance, and knowing, and the anxiety was coming from the misalignment that I was carrying deep within. My Soul wanted to speak. My human side needed to learn to listen to her.

My darkness was the suppression of my own inner wisdom and knowing, my Soul wisdom.

Slowly, slowly I began surrendering to her. Every day I learned to listen a bit more, tune in a bit more, decipher a bit more of this part of me that wanted to be heard. It was surprising to find that my anxiety seemed to lessen during this process. Now, every time before I start a client session, a meditation, a live or any group work I get still and ask her to step forward. I ask her to share her wisdom through me as a channel for my own inner wisdom. I still feel butterflies in my tummy today, but they are gone within a few minutes of opening my mouth. The fear and anxiety faded, and I am grateful for listening.

It was a huge revelation to realise that it was me suppressing my own inner voice. Yes, I had to go through the deep understanding of past lives and bad things that had happened to me, but the key factor that I had missed was that each and every one of us is Mind, Body and Soul. These 3 aspects of us need to work together. I am not just mind or body, Soul is always longing to be part of my expression here on Earth. She has chosen this body, and me, to come and share her light with the world, to share her gifts and wisdom with everyone out there.

Another key factor, one that I often see in the spiritual community, is the requirement to still our ego, something that I do not necessarily agree with. One of the biggest assets in my life and in my business is my super analytical over-thinking mind. The key difference for me is that I have learned to create a balance between my mind and my Soul. These two parts of me works together beautifully. Soul brings the creativity, the love and the expression, and mind takes this jumble of weirdness that floats around and forms it into a beautiful cohesive expression, a product, a course, or a book.

My question to you is – how are you putting Soul and Mind together? Have you taken the time to sit and understand what your Soul is wanting to express in this lifetime? How does that part of you want to show up in the world? And most importantly, are you allowing her to be heard?

I believe that through the process of self-exploration we are able to understand ourselves better, and we can uncover our hidden gifts. I would love to share some prompts with you to explore and to look at.

The journey of listening to our Soul starts with questioning our ideas, our beliefs, and the thought processes behind our thinking. The Soul wants you to unravel who you are now and rediscover your hidden gifts. Your Soul wants to shine and express in this life.

Here are some questions to ask yourself when it comes to authentic Soul expression:

- What in the world makes you happy? If I said to you today, you do not need to work another day in your life. You can do whatever you choose. What would you say?

- On a scale of 1 to 10 this thing/idea/concept that makes you happy – how much time do you spend doing it, working with it, connecting with it? (1 for no time at all and 10 being all the time)

- What is your excuse for not doing more of it?

- Are you afraid of what people would say if you allowed yourself to express your Soul?

- Why do you think you are afraid – judgement, guilt, shame, obligation, or fear?

Once you have honestly answered these questions, take some time to sit and investigate this part of you that you are not expressing. What would it feel like if you got to spend some time every week doing what makes you happy?

Close your eyes and take a moment to imagine yourself doing what makes you happy, feel in your gut what it feels like, how does it make your heart feel?

This for me was a great indicator of listening to my Soul. So, whenever I need to make a decision in my business or my life, I close my eyes, imagine what it would feel like once this decision has been made. If it feels heavy and constricted in my body, then I know it is not in alignment with my Soul need. However, when I close my eyes and I feel light as a feather, expansive and free I know that this is what my Soul wants to do, and I run towards it with all my might.

So, take some time now to start questioning yourself, your truth, and your beliefs. See how they go against what you feel deep inside that you want to express out there. We must unravel and heal ourselves so that we are able to share the beautiful Soul wisdom and love that we carry within. You will not regret it I promise!

Yolandi Boshoff - Soul Coach

You are here to create heaven on earth.

This is the story of every woman who feels lost and is searching for meaning and purpose. Who has lost touch with her divine essence and feels like a parched empty vessel, stuck, running on the treadmill of life, but not getting anywhere...

It was midnight and I could feel this huge heavy weight bearing down on me. I could not breathe. I tried to speak through snot and tears, "I can't do this! I can't live like this any longer!"

I was lying in bed, next to my then husband, where we lived in Texas. We had emigrated there from Edinburgh, Scotland with my seven-year-old son, after getting married. To all onlookers, it appeared like I was living the American dream minus the pool.

We had the holidays, the cars, motorbikes (yes, I had a bike, too), and friends. We went to live gigs, went sailing, and toasted marshmallows at the top of a live volcano in Guatemala. I know this sounds like the dream and our life appeared full, but I felt empty. I felt lost.

On the inside, I was crying out to be saved, to be happy, to find joy. To find my purpose. At this point, I just had not realised that I needed to save myself. I needed to return home to the divine truth; to the truth of my heart and soul's essence and to finally align my heart, body, and spirit.

I had been trying to feed the hungry ghost within my soul with the wrong things. With food, drink, drugs, overworking, and over-exercising. Undervaluing myself with inflated expectations of who I should be. In fact, I had basically spent my entire life searching outside myself for happiness, wholeness, love, and joy.

What I was yet to realise, was that the only thing that could satisfy this thirst, this yearning for purpose and something 'more than', was already there within me.

What was it that I could not do?

I thought it was live in Texas.
I thought if we just moved back to Edinburgh, I would be ok.
I thought if we just moved to California, I would be happy.
But happiness is an inside job, and I was about to learn that.

My thoughts, my beliefs, my own expectations were keeping me stuck.

I was keeping me stuck in an unhappy and unfulfilled groove, like an outdated needle on an old record player, you remember those? I was stuck repeating the same old bumpy groove.

I had to change!

I was put onto antidepressants for the 4th time, which did their thing to get me motivated and out of my icky funk, as well as brave enough to start on my path to finding myself. Yes, I was scared, but I chose to trust myself and the intuitive hits I was getting.

Do you know what the biggest game changer was? It was so simple.

I got quiet; I got my Zen on with meditation!! I became "Zen Iona."

Meditation actually saved my life. It was in surrendering to a greater power and trusting the divine that I came home to me and was able to start BEing me. Embracing the grace and power of BEing a divine Goddess. I found the connection within, that I had been searching for outside myself.

It was there all along, hidden in plain sight.

This connection to my essences goes by many names, Source of Universal Love, Mother Earth, Gaia, Your Higher Self, The Divine, The Great Oneness, Universe has your back, Buddha, Goddess, Your inner light, Wizard of Oz, or Bob. Call it what you will, as Shakespeare says "a rose by any other name would smell as sweet"

Meditation is listening—quieting the mind so that you hear the whispers of the Soul on the breeze, dancing across the ocean of infinite possibilities.

Now, I utterly sucked at both (Surrender and Meditation). I am not saying I had that "Hallelujah" moment . . . it was subtle, and I was NOW desperate. I felt there had to be something "more," and I was ready for it! I felt inspired and like an open channel.

As a rebellious teenager, I boycotted structured spiritual practices, running away from my hippie parents and their Buddhist paths. I had been blessed to be raised on a farm in the hills of Wales with FREEDOM, goats, hens, and horses. I 'now' thank them for giving me such a strong foundation in thinking outside the box in terms of spirituality, humanity, compassion, and unconditional love.

I knew we were different, and I did not like it.

I ran the other way into the arms of superficial/false salvation — self- sabotage and self-destruction, using alcohol, food, and drugs to fill the void in my soul. I had some fun (so much FUN), but I was left hungry and dissatisfied. I had been looking outside myself for all the resources I craved— in approval from others, my peer group, drink, drugs, partying, being loud and the centre of attention and even travelling to go find myself.

I had been there all along—as are you, there inside at your authentic core, your Heart, your Soul SELF as One with the Universe. Knowing this (at your core) will save you decades of searching. You are welcome.

This sense I had of being lost, restless and unfulfilled meant that my fears kept me stuck. My beliefs and fears of being judged as not enough, along with shame, guilt and unworthiness manifested as depression, anxiety, bulimia, addiction, lack of confidence and lack of self-belief.

Silently screaming from the inside, I knew without a shadow of a doubt that I had to calm the waters of my soul.

Once I became open to exploring my Truth, and uncovering my True North, like a needle on a compass I was magnetically drawn in the right direction. Coincidentally I started to discover amazing people in meditation groups, in the books that fell off shelves, and in chance encounters at the coffee shop. We do not need to look at the why or the how; just trust, have faith, and fall forwards back home to yourself.

The path started with Meditation and led me to a remembering, awakening and awareness of my Soul Medicine gifts. Along the way, I embraced Energy Healing, Ancestral Lineage Clearing, Chinese medicine, Chakra Vibrations, Oracle cards, Heart Healing, Starseeds, Lightworkers, Goddesses, Quantum Physics, New Thought Leaders, Quantum field healing and Integrative Health—to name a few of the areas that interested me—plus my own gifts, of course.

"Change the Way You Look At Things, and the Things You Look At Change" - Wayne Dyer

I became inspired through meditation, and it felt SOOOO GOOOD. I had to continue with MORE of this. It became an integral part of my life and not a "thing" I had to do. My husband at the time referred to my transformation as "Zen Iona." I became calmer and a much less shouty mum. I found inner peace and was not triggered as much by other peoples 'actions as I had been before. This is how "Zen Iona" and my true calling for empowering others came into being.

The truth is that I have always wanted to lift others up. But when I was younger, I did not know that it was my calling, my passion. It simply came naturally.

When I was a child, I am told I played with the kids excluded by others. I have volunteered, worked in areas that created positive change in charities, advocacy work and legal policy change. I have loved so much of what I did but something was always missing.

There is one thing that stays true throughout these callings. No matter who you are, where you are from, or your personal circumstances, you can change. I could not change the system, but I could change the hearts and souls of those I worked with. No matter where you are in your business you can have a bigger impact, and if you have not started yet, then start now.

It is my purpose to help ignite and align the hearts and souls of all those who feel the call to create change and impact in their lives and the lives of others.

You can have an aligned soulful, fulfilling life with an abundance of joy and success in all areas—home, love, business, family, relationships. I know because I have done it and so have my clients.

Know this: It is possible to reinvent yourself from the inside out and live the Life you were born to live with joy, ease, and flow. It is possible to break through that self-imposed glass ceiling. It is possible to align with your divine purpose and live your legacy now.

My journey back home to myself, to BEing whole and complete as One with the Universe, meant looking at the world through a fresh lens. For a long time, what was missing was ME, and that feeling of oneness. I invite you, the reader, to find yourself a cheerleader and challenger of the soulful kind to guide you on your voyage and align heart, body, and spirit. Who are you surrounding yourself with? What podcasts are you listening to? What books are you reading?

Are you feeling inspired and are you living in the vibration of LOVE?

We are either living in Fear or Love, and when we are not living from a place of love, we are calling for Love. We all have innate wellbeing, health, and happiness within us. We have just forgotten. We have forgotten who we were before "they" told us who to be. Before we told ourselves how to be. Before we put on the Mask of conformity and hid behind it.

We can choose to transform our lives by "realigning" ourselves to who we are at our core, our Heart, on a Soul level, back to our authentic Self. Remembering who we are—the wild and gifted wise woman, soul siSTAR—a Spiritual being having a human experience. It is time for you to Shine Bright and BE Magnificent!

Release the story you have held onto, let go of the external exceptions, transmute fear into love. It is all energy, everything, so what energy are you amplifying.

When the flow of energy in our being is blocked, this discomfort reveals itself as limiting and negative thoughts, emotions, and behaviours.

Embark on your Heart led journey of soulful discovery by releasing the negative thinking, habits and limiting beliefs that have kept you feeling "stuck". Find inspiration all around you in magical daily musings, meditation, joy, walking, creativity, dancing - do whatever will help release unwanted feelings of low self-esteem, lack, and judgment, as well as outdated myths and fears.

You can learn to surf the rise and fall of life's waves of adversity and triumph. Recognise your magnificence, your precious gifts, and move confidently toward your purpose, passion, and joy. Awaken the light within and live with ease, grace, and authenticity.

Happiness and Joy are not destinations we reach if we ignore the storms, the negativity, the dark and the shadows. Happiness is about weathering the storm, going through adversity, learning from it, and creating opportunities and infinite possibilities from it.

You are here to create heaven on earth.
You are here to live your truth.

"The Path to Divine embodiment, inspiration and alignment is a simple one of Joy."

You may well ask "how the heck do I begin this epic quest?"

Let us start at the beginning. What brings you Joy?

For me, it is the simple things—a walk in the sunshine, hearing my son laugh, breathing deeply by the ocean, a book that I cannot put down, playing board games with my son...

What brings you joy? Follow your Joy!

If what you are doing does not light you up, if it does not light your Soul on Fire, STOP doing it. Do what lights you up!

Do what inspires you.
Try something you have always wondered about doing.

Follow your curiosity—you just might be surprised at where it leads.

Find your limits and push through them to Joy!

A Peaceful Practice:
Divide a sheet of paper in half.
On one side, make a list of all the things you enjoy doing.
On the other side, make a list of all the things you are curious about trying. Look at the lists.
Keep adding to them.

Go out and do something that you enjoy.

Iona Russell – Intuitive Mindset Coach

Awakening the Divine within.

"Not enough"

It was the refrain that ran through my mind whatever I tried to do. They were the words that led me to work long hours at jobs where I did well, but came home feeling drained, unfulfilled, and even disrespected; the ones that led me to drink on nights out until I did not feel "boring" anymore; and those that sent me into friendships and relationships where I was so focused on the other person's needs that I forgot about and betrayed my own.

And that sentiment was not just one I heard on the inside, but one that rang out loud and clear from the outside world too. I saw it in the photos of airbrushed celebrities that graced magazines and billboards, in the adverts that told me all the ways I should be spending money to become somehow better and in the ways the world rolled its eyes at me because I had not yet checked off all the boxes in the Game of Life-style checklist society gives us for happiness.

I would like to tell you that one day I looked in the mirror and saw myself as the Goddess I am, but the truth is almost the opposite; that one day I got tired of feeling shitty, exhausted, and burdened, drained from reading and talking about the Divine Feminine while feeling anything but that myself.

I decided it was time to put down the books that promised sure fire strategies for happiness, and step away from the teachers who assured me that their model was the guaranteed way to empowerment, and instead connect with the person who knew me better than anyone... me.

Fast forward five years and while life is not perfect, it is nourishing, fulfilling, healthy and joy filled. I find myself putting my phone in another room while I take an evening – or even a whole afternoon – to relax and do something fun without the anxiety of anything I should be reading or responding to; dancing like a wild woman on nights out even though it's been over three years since my last drink; and setting the kind of boundaries in relationships that mean I can support the people I love without feeling miserable and drained and while having my needs met too.

All because I made a choice to turn inwards, and to question and listen to what I heard there until it led me back to that divine spark, I had heard so much about.

It sounds simple doesn't it? After all, "listen to your inner voice" is said so often nowadays it has become a bit of a cliché. But like so many of the things we are told regularly without context, it is often not that easy – especially when we are so often told that the voice within us might not be so divine after all.

We live in such a noisy world, and one that works so hard to not only distract us from ourselves but also to convince us that inner voice cannot be trusted – and for good reason. Because once we reconnect with that divine spark that lives within us, we start to reclaim our power over life and the world around us. We stop looking outside of ourselves for validation and stop spending money on all the things that claim to drown out that voice of "not enoughness". Instead, we remember the path to fulfilment all on our own.

One of the wisest pieces of guidance I have ever received came to me when I was channelling spirit for a client around the time of my self-reconnection: "You are a human being, not a human doing; the clue has always been in the name." Sounds basic right? But for me it felt incredibly revolutionary.

So, when I speak of stepping away from those distractions, that is a big part of what I mean... Stepping out of the doing and allowing ourselves the time to simply be and reconnect with what we find there. For me that journey meant a lot of walking amongst the trees and listening to the birds, and just as much time on a meditation cushion or cosying up under a blanket with my dog and the kind of book that brings me joy. These are things that help me to feel aligned, whole, and grateful to be alive, but more than that, they are the things that helped me remember who I really was before I tried to be something else.

Of course, once we do find ways to be away from the outside noise and the pulls to do, there is a different kind of noise we have to contend with; those shadows, shames, and fears that all too often run wild inside of our minds with the same fervour as my "not enough" message.

I know, those are the exact things that we all work so hard to drown out and avoid. But on the quest to re-awaken and reconnect with our own divinity, they are exactly the things we need to pay attention to. Why? Because they are the monsters that guard the treasure of our divine sparks.

Many people out there will tell you the secret to reconnecting with your divinity is in ignoring those shadows and focusing solely on your own glorious light. That sounds wonderful, but in my experience, it is just not true. The secret to overcoming those monsters is always in getting to know them; in paying attention to what they are so afraid of and then working through each of those things.

That can take some time, because often those divine sparks of ours are the very things we have been shamed, shunned, and mocked for; those we have been told to turn away from and those that do not quite fit in the cookie cutter lives the outside world would like us to live.

But here is the first thing you learn when you reconnect with your own divine spark: That the secret to a fulfilled life is never one lived solely on someone else's terms; it is one in which you can be truly and wholly yourself.

Make no mistake, that can be scary. Some of my favourite words ever written were by Marianne Williamson, who said:
"Our deepest fear is not that we are inadequate. Our deepest fear is that we are powerful beyond measure. It is our light, not our darkness that most frightens us. We ask ourselves, 'Who am I to be brilliant, gorgeous, talented, fabulous?' Actually, who are you not to be?"

Let me ask that again; who are you not to be? Really? Outside of all the bullshit society has sold you in its attempt to keep you small.

I know, I know, you might well be shaking your head right now and saying something along the lines of "it's easy for *you* to say that, you don't know me!" That is true.

But I know the journey I have been on, and I have had the honour of supporting enough clients through journeys of their own to trust in the fact that you are brilliant, gorgeous, talented, and fabulous and that your own divine spark is in there just waiting to be re-ignited.

So how do we connect with and awaken that divine part of you?

To me there are four simple ways to start:

Get grounded.
This is where the walking in the woods came in for me, but grounding looks different for everyone. It is about bringing yourself truly into the here and now; remembering that although you are an infinitely wise and powerful soul, you are also human, and bringing yourself back into your human body and this glorious planet – the place where you are fortunate enough to be able to express that divine spark of yours – every moment of every day.

One of the easiest ways I like to do this is to close my eyes and breathe deeply for a moment. As I inhale, I imagine roots growing – huge, thick roots like those of an old tree – which sprout out of my solar plexus and stretch right down into the centre of the earth until I can feel the pulse that beats there. On the exhale, I imagine a glorious bright light coming out of the top of my head and stretching up into the stars; all the way up until I feel held by my ancestors and by the wisdom of the whole Universe.

Get quiet.
Turn off the TV, put down the books and step away from the other people who like to have their say; then tune into that inner voice of yours. Maybe you do this through meditation or maybe you are someone who would rather keep their hands or body busy by running, gardening or something similar – whatever you need to be able to do to hear the insight that exists under the outside noise and mental chatter, this is all about being able to hear yourself think... and then paying attention to what you find here.

Own your shit.

When those less than comfortable voices make themselves heard it is time for us to get familiar with them. We do this by working through the painful experiences of our past – not only in this lifetime but in those we have lived before that have left their own scars on our souls; and in the experiences of our ancestors that have been carried forward in our genes and in the ways we have been raised. We work to process and heal those experiences a part of us is so terrified of repeating; to break the patterns that have been keeping us small and to own those things that we know are not quite so bright and shiny but are nonetheless part of our own divine power and wisdom.

This is about confronting those monsters of ours and helping them understand that accessing the treasure they are so dutifully guarding is not a dangerous path to destruction and persecution, but something to be encouraged – a path to wholeness which will bring peace for them as much as for you.

Own your spark.

One of my favourite exercises to do with clients is in asking them for all the labels they carry – job titles, relationships to other people and things they do. Once they have listed all of those things, I ask them a second question: "Now who are you underneath all of that?"

The answer inevitably involves things and places they love, activities that make them feel most like themselves and their core values – the drivers that help them to keep going and push for something better in everything that they do.

At the root of all of that we tend to find something incredible: the divine spark that has been lighting them up from the inside all along, just waiting to be found and to light us up with that beautiful feelings of knowing just who we are. And while that spark may not have all the answers on what they should *do* next, it has a damned good way of showing them how to *be*. And it is that which, in its own special way, inevitably leads them step by step to the wholeness and fulfilment they were looking for all along.

Ceryn Rowntree – Soul-Led Therapist

You are here to enjoy, create, love and be loved.

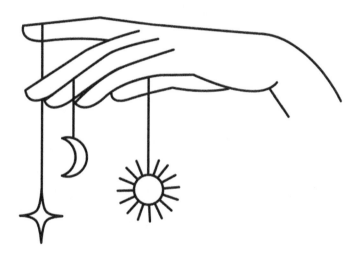

"Love is the greatest healing power I know. Love can heal even the deepest and most painful memories because love brings the light of understanding to the darkest corners of our hearts and minds."
-Louise Hay

Love is our superpower. We just have to tap into the love within.

Give the love that you desire to yourself, and love will come back to you. Self-love is the most important love that we can give in my opinion. Without love of self, we cannot truly love others.

We are born in this amazing vessel we call the human body. We experience the perfection of it every day. We do not need to tell it how to function because it knows what to do. The heart beats, the lungs expand and the blood flows while we move about our daily lives. Shades and textures of skin and hair unique to every single living thing. I could go on and on about this beautiful temple in which we live.

There is beauty all around us but there comes a time when we will need to look beyond all of the beautiful flesh and see and feel the incredible spirit within. Our spirit selves. Source, Universe, God, the Light within. The Spirit within you that knows and loves you unconditionally. The Self that loves you for who you are flaws and all. The Self that feels satisfaction, pleasure, and ecstasy. The feeling of peace and wellbeing. That is the essence of God, and that Love energy is in every single living thing.

This pure love within can also hear our thoughts and self-talk. We have over 6,000 thoughts per day and those thoughts become the things we see around us. When I became consciously aware of my thoughts, I knew I had to make a change. I had to start with asking myself some important questions.

Am I speaking words of Love to myself?
Am I speaking words of Love to my body?
Am I speaking words of Love into my life?

My thoughts had been out of control and my life was evidence of that. I had created all of this pain and could not run from it anymore. I had been married and divorced in less than three years, and my current relationship was falling apart. I carried so much guilt and shame within me. My physical body had been affected by my thoughts as well. When I started the journey to love myself, I was 34 years old with a history of fibroid and asthma, unsure if I would ever have children. I was angry and broken and my inner dialogue reflected that.

If I wanted my life to be different, I had to change my thinking and open my heart. I had to start with me. If I wanted to heal, I knew I had to stop focusing on everyone else and look within. If I wanted to experience unconditional love, I had to give it to myself.

Once I made the choice to look within, I was introduced to Science of Mind and Universal Law. This was the connection of mind body and Spirit I had been looking for all my life. It had been inside of me all along. I discovered the book "You can Heal your Life" from Louise Hay and I was obsessed.

I came to the realization that I could heal my life, and that everything I needed was within me. Not separate in the sky somewhere, but right inside of me. Vibrating and tingling throughout my body. I also began my journey to heal my womb with tantric massage. The Source of life itself blossoms from my womb. The same womb that had to be cleared of trauma, unforgiveness, shame and guilt. I had to address my inner child and be there for her when I felt like no one else was. I had to go deep within, to repair the deep hurts from my childhood and early adulthood.

Generational curses and race consciousness that ran deep in my subconscious mind required reprogramming, in order to become my higher self. My focus was beyond the surface and labels, because ultimately, I am a spiritual being. We All are spiritual beings.

Self-love was the only way for me to heal from the trauma that had started to manifest physically in my body. I had nothing to lose and everything to gain. My physical, mental, and spiritual health and wellbeing was and will always be my priority.

I forgave myself and others for everything that had happened in my life. This took some work, but the freedom was well worth it. Unforgiveness kept up a steady stream of negative thoughts that literally did not feel good. Eventually I could see the blessing and opportunity for expansion. Forgiveness is for your own freedom of bondage within your mind and body.

I started connecting with my inner being as often as possible, through meditation and quieting the mind. Being in nature with my family is medicine for me and a form of meditation. Yoga helped as well with connecting my mind, body, and spirit. Dancing and music are my favorite healing rituals.

I replaced negative thoughts that were becoming negative things in my life with thoughts of love to heal. With daily affirmations (love deposits) and practice my thoughts quickly began to change for the better. I became lighter and a sense of knowing replaced the hopelessness.

I continue to heal and ignite my life force and celebrate my wonderful womb. I had to become the lover and partner that I wanted to attract in my life. I stopped looking for things to accuse or blame my husband and anyone else from my past for. I stopped reminding myself and my husband of ways that he hurt me. And I started focusing on what unconditional love felt like, one day at a time. The past was over, and I was still madly in love with this man. But if I wanted the type of relationship with him that I knew was possible, I had to take responsibility for my part in the destruction of our past relationship.

We had both shown our shadow selves to each other and under all of the pain and hurt we still loved each other and wanted to create a different story together. We coached each other but stayed focused on our own personal journey. We got to the zero point of our relationship, so we knew the only way from here was up.

I noticed that the more loving I was to myself the more loving I was to everyone else. And in return, others were nicer to me and that was a win - win. My husband and I practice tantric energy massage on each other to remove any blocks and to really begin to connect from the heart. I began igniting my womb and allowing myself to be truly vulnerable with someone. We became the lovers we always were looking for. I celebrate Shakti and dance to ignite my life force. The feminine divine Goddess of pure potential became alive within me.

Self-love has become a daily practice and way of life for me and it is reflected in my life. I trust myself and my relationships have a deeper connection. I love my body more and more every day. I am honored to be the Mother of three amazing children and two bonus children that I love and adore. Plant medicine has helped me in so many wonderful ways. The herbs, plants, fruit, and flowers of the earth are here to help us during this time of healing and discovery. I am abundant in love and loving friendships. There is peace that has come over me and I feel reborn and enlightened. I know that I am creating my reality and I do not look outside of myself anymore for acceptance. We all are here to experience our own unique journey to expansion.

Here are a few things you can do to begin your journey to healing and self-love.

- Begin a daily routine to quiet your mind at least once a day. That could be meditation, a walk-in nature, yoga, or whatever you do to slow down and be present in the moment.

- Move your body in ways that feel good and give you pleasure. Dance with yourself.

- Trust yourself. You have all the answers.

- Connect with Mother Nature and the Moon. The energy exchange from our planet is essential.

- Speak Love on yourself and others. Stop complaining and make the necessary changes to be happy and joyous.

- Forgive, Forgive and Forgive!!!!

- Make Love and discover your sensual sacred self! You are worthy of Love! And if you do not have a partner be your own Lover! Find all of the delicious places you can take yourself.

- Listen to music that aligns you with love. Music is therapeutic and connects us to a feeling. Choose music that makes you feel good.

"Love is the great miracle cure. Loving ourselves works miracles in our lives."
-Louise Hay
You are here to enjoy, create, love and be loved! The answers you seek are within you.

Change is not always easy, but living a life of hurt, pain and dis-ease is even harder. You have nothing to lose (except limitations) and everything to gain. I believe in you!

Peace and Love,
Infiniti Jones

Infiniti Jones – Goddess of healing sound and love

Guided by my Spirit team.

As I sit here linking to my Spiritual Guides, I feel a true sense of knowing that I am exactly where I am meant to be at this stage of my life. However, it has not always been like that...

Before starting out on my spiritual journey I felt as if I was floating through life, not really knowing where I was heading, not sure who I was. I did not have an easy childhood. I was bullied at school, partly because of a horrid skin condition called eczema, and partly because I did not feel like I fitted in. I did not do well at school and I could not wait to leave.

When I did, I worked in many different areas of business, Accounts, Management, Business Analysis, and Business Coaching. The organisations I worked for varied, from small one-man businesses, through to multinational corporates. In one of my previous jobs, I managed a team and found myself being bullied again. Although I was reasonably successful in my career, it did not bring me any satisfaction. I had no sense of purpose, felt no passion for my work, and I felt lost, with no sense of belonging. This created the limiting belief that I was not good enough. I had no confidence and no self-belief.

Around 25 years ago, after a couple of awful years, I started searching for something. I did not know what I was looking for, but I knew when I found it, I would know.

I started an aromatherapy course. On the last day of the course, couple of the other ladies told me that there was a really good medium living close to me and gave me her number. I decided I would ring her that night to book a reading. When I rang, she said to me "I'm running a course tomorrow and I really feel you should come on it," I asked what kind of course and she said it was to develop psychic and mediumship skills. I had never thought of attending anything like this, however, I was curious just felt right.

For once I listened to that intuitive voice calling out to me.

I went on the course and it was amazing. I knew I had found that something I was looking for. This was my path, the start of my spiritual journey, and what a phenomenally magical and wonderful journey it is. I finally found my purpose and passion.

Once I started out on this journey, the synchronicities began, new spiritual opportunities were revealed along the way, as and when I was ready for them, and I rarely had to go looking for them, they usually presented themselves

My mentor and teacher was a remarkable and very wise lady. Definitely the right teacher for me. Keen to develop my skills further, I joined her development group and attended many of her workshops. She opened many doors and knocked down many of the barriers I had built up.

I suffered with Imposter Syndrome. Who the hell did I think I was? Why would spirit choose me as their communicator? But they did, and the quality of communication I had with them was phenomenal. My mentor believed in me though, and that drove me further forward; although it took a little longer for me to believe in myself, and I was slower than many others to take the leap to begin serving spiritualist churches and doing 1-2-1 readings for people.

The first step of my spiritual journey was learning to meditate. What a wonderful technique, allowing oneself to be energetically open to receive guidance and communication from the higher realms. Of course, as I expanded and grew spiritually, I began to understand how much more there is to energy and consciousness than meets the eye; a mesmerizing subject that I continue to research.

I was introduced to trance work and this helped me strengthen the connection with my Guides, to link in and allow their wisdom to flow through me. Initially when I started, I would wake up at stupid o'clock, 2 or 3 in the morning with an overwhelming urge to write! As I could not get back to sleep, I would think that I needed to get the words out of my head and onto paper; I wrote reams of words from spirit, the words just flowed, words that were not my words but beautiful words of the universal energies of love and joy.

This work helped to re-enforce my belief in my guides, to understand more about the realms of spirit and how it worked. I was learning to trust and believe in that power greater than myself and it was fascinating.

The more I work with my Guides & Helpers, the stronger my intuition becomes. Intuition is that feeling of knowing something is right. You do not really know how you know; you just know. It is hard to trust because it cannot always be backed up with a logical argument. At first, I did not really understand how intuition worked, I thought the things that happened were just co-incidences, but of course there is no such thing.

I asked my guides to help me to understand it, here is the guidance I received from them:

"Awareness of intuition can come in many different ways, it depends on the individual's awareness and which of their senses are the strongest, some of the methods are as follows:

- Meditation allows the mind to slow down. This can often result in what may appear to be random thoughts, but if you look at them in more detail, you can see that they are intuitive thoughts.
- You may get a feeling in your gut; some people will feel it in their heart centre.
- You just know something, but you do not know why. For example, a friend is upset or ill and you feel compelled to ring or contact them.
- You may have dreams that you know are correct.
- Patterns or signs may appear to you. Perhaps you are thinking of studying a new subject but need to decide on what. Adverts and articles on a subject may show up where you least expect them to.
- You have been looking for a particular item for your home and have not been able to find it. On a day out you suddenly feel inspired to go into a shop that is not your usual choice, low and behold there is the item you have been looking for, the exact thing you wanted.

I often regret the times I ignore my intuition. One day when I was leaving work, I had a strong sense that I should take a different route home. I ignored that feeling and 3.5 hours later I arrived home! There had been a major accident on my main route home and the traffic was gridlocked for hours.

When I do listen to that intuitive voice, I am amazed. One evening I was driving home from running a development group, as I approached the traffic lights they had just changed to amber, as I went to put my foot down, I heard a very loud voice saying STOP. I slammed my brakes on and as I did, I noticed a car at the other junction had jumped their amber light; had I not stopped there would have been a very bad accident.

There are many ways of improving that awareness, see my free course and meditation, Introduction to Intuition.

Eventually I started doing readings and felt blessed that I could share messages from the spirit world. Messages affirming their love, bringing such joy and relief to the recipient. Confirming that their loved ones were okay. I started to serve in Spiritualist Churches where I linked with my Guides to bring through philosophy / words of wisdom, I gave messages to the congregation and felt honoured that I could do this work.

I began teaching my own groups and discovered that I loved being able to support others on their learning journey, helping give them the confidence and self-belief that they needed. I understood when they doubted that they could do it, when they were scared to get it wrong. I had been there. One thing I had recognised was that often our greatest learning comes from getting it wrong and recognising how to go back and think outside of the box, creating a new and often unique way of teaching. I am very fortunate knowing that my guides support me and lead me in the right direction.

My Spiritual Coaching came about after being contacted by an ex-colleague, who amazed me by thanking me for inspiring him to start up his own business. He told me he had a coaching & mentoring business, and he recalled that I had previously set up a programme for an organisation of over 250 people and how amazing it had been.

I knew then that I would use my 25+ years' experience as a Coach and Mentor to help others find their Spiritual self, their own true purpose.

I have encountered many lessons in life. Including learning to love self. Until we start to do that, how can we possibly learn to love others. It is not easy to turn off that inner critic, that voice that shouts loudly that you are not good enough. But each time it shouts, replace it with a something positive about yourself. Believe me there are so many more positive things than you can initially think of.

Learning to trust your intuition can be majorly transformational. Practice it, keep a journal and identify how it works for you. You may not always get it right in the beginning, but as you practice, the feeling will become easier to trust and you will get it right more often. The more you trust it, the more empowered you become.

Our intuition has always been there, many of us have just forgotten how to tune into it; intuition will speak to you in a way that you understand. It may be a feeling in your gut or simply a knowing. You will work out your own intuitive language.
Albert Einstein was a true advocate of intuition, he stated:

"The intuitive mind is a sacred gift, and the rational mind is a faithful servant. We have created a society that honors the servant and has forgotten the gift."

Intuition could be called "knowing without knowing why", "thinking with your heart" or "gut feeling."
And "I believe in intuitions and inspirations... I sometimes FEEL that I am right. I do not KNOW that I am."

Steve Jobs stated: "Intuition is a very powerful thing, more powerful than intellect."

He said that intuition was responsible for the Apple phone and tablet.

Have the courage to follow your heart and intuition. They already know what you truly want to become. Everything else is secondary.

Some years ago, I had a very powerful intuitive feeling. I felt it was time to move back to the North East, back to my roots, the sea and the countryside, time to live my purpose. We had not discussed it, but I said to my husband that he should look for a job in the North, he was offered one within two weeks. We put our house on the market and it sold immediately.

We found a house to move to and put in an offer which was accepted. Within 2.5 months we had moved into our dream house, 5 minutes from the beach and 10 minutes from the North Yorkshire moors, a place of outstanding beauty.

Once we moved, I started developing my Spiritual business on a full-time basis instead of the hobby it had been. My life is so different now, I am so much happier, and I love what I do, I live in a state of joy and gratitude. My belief system has shown me that there is so much more to our life than we know. I know that life continues after our earthly existence. This has been proven to me so many times with communication from spirit.

Wendy Dixon – Spiritual Coach & Psychic Medium

Goddess, Who me?

"Look at YOU, YOU are so out of shape, what's wrong with YOU, YOU know better, YOU were an athlete, get your $h!t together.". I am pretty sure these are not Goddess powered thoughts. This was just another moment of my life where I jumped on that shame train to Loserville.

Another moment where I judged and bullied myself. It was also one of the most transformational moments in my life.

My husband and I had recently moved to Florida and I joined the local YMCA so I could lap swim. I found myself at the pool. It was midday, due to my schedule and errands I needed to run. I stood at the edge of the pool stretching, putting on my cap and goggles like I had done thousands of times before, as a former Olympic trial qualifying swimmer in the 1970's. Enjoying the moment, the sun, the warmth, watching all the other lap swimmers do their thing.

I jumped in the water, pushed off the wall and felt the freedom and joy I experience when I swim. I got to the other end, did a flip turn, pushed off the wall and a rush of thoughts entered my mind. No longer was I experiencing joy, peace, and freedom, instead my inner mean girl turned up, to remind me of all the things that were wrong with me. "YOU are so out of shape...YOU have no discipline... YOU are such a loser... etc." What felt like a pummeling of negative thoughts filled my head and heart within seconds, I had not even made it to the middle of the pool.

Then something miraculous happened. I caught myself in the act. The act of bullying myself and the moment that I jumped on that damn shame train. I screamed in my head, to her, "Out of shape for WHO? For WHAT? I'm not training for the Olympics!".

At that moment I chose to take my power back. I chose to talk back to my inner mean girl (I now call her Trixie, she tries to trick me into believing nonsense) who, by the way, had been a "faithful" companion of mine for many decades. In that moment I chose self-compassion and gratitude. I rolled over on my back, felt the sun on my face, and I began to think, "I am so grateful to be living in Florida, to be here at this pool, in the middle of the day, enjoying a swim and the sun.

I am so grateful that my husband was willing to take a transfer because he knew that after 30 years away, I would love to live near the beach. I am grateful for my health and that I can swim. Because about 5 years ago, I was quite ill and had to quit swimming and (swim) coaching. Who cares if I have gained some weight, I am healthy, strong, I paddle board, I walk the beach, and my husband loves me just the way I am." All of this happened while I swam a single length of the pool. This is the power of our mind. All day long. It has the power to take us out of the game or the power to help us live in our truth.

I share this story, because it was not until I turned 50 (yes, 50) that I truly heard the message that my thoughts create feelings, which drive actions, which create results. I was learning about paradigms, belief systems and universal laws. I was learning that I was the creator of my life, my suffering, and yes that also meant I was the creator of my joy and success as well. My mind was blown. Where had this been my whole life. I needed to know this when I was ten years old. And up until that day at the pool, I had been a victim of my thinking, not a victim of my circumstances like I wanted to believe. My thoughts and beliefs were so pervasive that it took me some time to learn how to think new thoughts (I got help to do that, changing your brain is not easy) and to become the observer of my mind. When I did, my whole world began to change.

So, where do all these thoughts come from anyway? Such a powerful question. I used to just believe everything in my head. These are my thoughts, they are in my head, they must be me.

Nope! You are not your thoughts. You are the creator of your thoughts. You are the thinker of your thoughts. Afterall, who is it that is noticing the thoughts. That is the real YOU.

Like you, I was not born with any thoughts or beliefs. I inherited them from my parents and family. I learned them from adults, my peers and society. I created many of them from traumatic events, and life experiences.

I am not good enough, I am unworthy, I am not the right size, I am a fraud, I am not good with money, I do not make good decisions, I am not loveable. No one cares what I have to say. I am no Goddess. Just a few of the beliefs that I carried with me.

This brings me to this book project and title of this chapter. Goddess, Who me? The word goddess triggered me. Maybe it triggers you too. I almost didn't take part. I almost "believed" that I was not a right fit for this book. Who calls themselves a goddess? What is an everyday goddess anyway? I didn't get it. Why would someone want to be a goddess? It seemed so airy-fairy, whimsical, flighty, all feminine energy, all the flow, and just mythology (get your head out of the clouds).

For years (ok decades) I was so full of self-criticism and self-loathing that of course I was judging other women who owned their truth, power, and femininity. I was too busy trying to be an Alpha Female, to be in control, trying to achieve my way out of my unworthiness. I was too busy living life as a human-DOING and not a human-BEING. I was too busy avoiding my feelings. Too busy overthinking, overeating, overdrinking, overworking, over volunteering, overspending, over doing and overachieving. I was too busy to stop sleepwalking through life, so my body did it for me.

I was a good woman doing good work in the world. I was a successful nurse, champion swim coach, loving wife, mom, leader but inside I was struggling with unworthiness and imposter syndrome.

C.S. Lewis says, "We are who we believe we are". This is NOT the truth of who we are, it is simply what we have chosen to believe consciously and unconsciously. The truth is we are powerful, spiritual beings. I chose to believe all those lies about myself for decades because I did not know there was another way. I just thought this is me... and I felt powerless to change it. Until I learned otherwise.

When my health began to suffer, that is when I had to start letting go of control all the things. What people said, how they would feel, what they would think, what they did or did not do. Worrying about stuff that most likely would not even happen. I began connecting to myself and tapping into what I did have control over. My thoughts, my feelings, my actions, my results, and my intuition. My purpose, my wisdom, my dreams, my desires, and my truth.

This was not an easy shift, my ego fought hard to stay in charge. I immersed myself in learning about thought work, mindset, beliefs, and trauma. I worked with master coaches and healers in order to find my truth, my purpose, my peace of mind.

For me this "wake up call" or midlife awakening as I like to call it (oh there were many I did not listen to along the way) was when I decided something had to change. I decided it was me! I needed a new way to think and to be. And I had no idea where to start.

I decided I would figure it out. I started. Since 2008, there have been five major things I did to change my life and create a remarkable second act (ok it's more like my 22nd act but who's counting). While I would love to call them steps, I have discovered that because I am a living, breathing, spiritual being having a human experience, I am always working with these elements in my life, which is why I love teaching them because they are the skills you will use the rest of your life.

- Reimagining my future and deciding that I wanted to be well. What else did I want? Why did I want to be healthy? Asking myself those questions showed me something and while I did not vision myself as a Goddess, I did imagine myself happy, healthy, and worthy and able to travel, paddle board, etc.

- Reclaiming my Health. PCOS, auto-immune colitis, depression, becoming -gluten, dairy, corn, alcohol, and sugar free. I became a gut health expert.

- Rewiring my mind by learning powerful thought work tools. You can start with journaling your thoughts, beginning to notice what is going on in your head. Practice the acronym W.A.I.T. What Am I Thinking? When you feel upset, scared, anxious, overwhelmed, or angry, notice the sentences in your mind. Choose a new more empowering thought.

- Reframing my past through trauma work. I especially love E4Trauma Method®, for reframing your limiting beliefs. It is most helpful to do this with a trained practitioner (like me), or a counselor who can support you while you process these experiences. You can start by simply completing this statement; "I am afraid to write that book because.... I am upset with myself because..." Have compassion for what comes up and try not to judge yourself.

- Reconnecting with myself. This has been both the most challenging and the most powerful. I believe we all crave connection (even before the pandemic), and what we are craving the most is this connection to our intuition, our higher self, our source of all that is. It is in this knowing and this truth that I have found my peace and my purpose. Mindfulness and meditation, even if it is only for a couple of minutes.

Embracing this work (yes, it is work but it is worth it) has created true transformation in every area of my life.

- My relationships are great because I am no longer people pleasing or shape shifting. I work to no longer judge them; I am rarely triggered. I choose to love them on their journey and use boundaries when I feel the need, Stay connected and in community.
- I live with vitality, health, and wellbeing. I travel, swim, hike, paddle board, and I no longer use food, alcohol, or anything else to numb out instead I know how to process my thoughts and feelings.
- My beliefs about money, prosperity and my worthiness have given us financial freedom. My husband and I moved to Florida, built our dream house, creating our best life.
- My "knowing" the truth of who I AM, my freedom of expression, and creativity gives me the goddess power to live my purpose and calling as a speaker, teacher, author coach and podcaster and why not, Alpha-Goddess the best of both worlds.

Nearly ten years after my mom had passed, she came to me in spirit and said, "WAKE UP JUDY, WAKE UP... YOU'VE GOT WORK TO DO... MAKE YOUR MESS YOUR MESSAGE." I began to cry, and asked her, "Which mess, which message, there are so many". And that has been my mission since 2015. Cleaning up my messes, finding the messages and sharing with other women trying to find peace and purpose themselves.

We are on a constant journey of reinvention, of unbecoming and becoming. If nothing else from this chapter speaks to you, I want to leave you with this powerful message.

- Do not believe everything you think (most are lies unless you have mastered your mind)
- Question every thought and belief (do your trauma work)
- Do not doubt that You are a GOD(ESS) because you are the "I AM".
- You are never too old, and it is never too late, to Get Your Second (or 22nd) Act Together!

Judy Prokopiak – Resilience & Spiritual Coach

Reclaim your self-care Goddess.

Stepping into Goddessdom is something I never imagined would be part of my life's journey, and I am honored to be here.

In the spirit of full disclosure, the word Goddess has not always sat well with me. I was judgmental without knowing the facts. I worried about labels, boxes, typecasting, and people compromising their emotional and spiritual beliefs to belong in a community. I now know differently; a Goddess is someone who embraces their personal power, follows their heart, and reaches for the stars. Not scared of failing or falling short.

A Goddess is someone who embraces their true north through self-care. As a Yoga & Spiritual teacher, it is my life's mission to inspire people to follow their hearts and find something that sparks joy in every part of their being. There are no shortcuts or magic pills you can take that make it easier. It takes hard work, consistency, and time. It is genuinely only possible when we become accountable for our feelings and take affirmative action to change our lives.

Finding your true north through self-care sounds easy, doesn't it? It sounds like something we should all be doing all the time, a no brainer. We live in a society where we feel obliged to always care for others. From an early age we are told to always look after others, often to our own detriment. It may never be said out loud, but it is an unspoken expectation in our society.

We often feel that taking time for ourselves is selfish, a luxury. Any free time we have should be used to get ahead of ourselves; maybe catch up with some ironing or another task that benefits others.

If I ever feel guilty for taking time for me, I think about my amazing Mum. She left a toxic and abusive marriage with three kids, and she was not even thirty years old. She worked like a dog to keep us fed, watered and safe but never took time for herself. Ultimately, later in life it broke her, and she suffered from chronic mental health problems for several years. My Mum's struggle and sacrifice have inspired me to always take care of myself and not feel guilty when I take time for me.

Her utter devotion to her family was beautiful, and I am eternally grateful for everything. It taught me that realistically, we cannot run forever. At some point it will catch up with us. We will feel the wrath of self-neglect. I know self-neglect is a big statement, but that is what it is in a nutshell.

If you focus everything on everyone else, something has to give. We are not super-human, no matter what we think. We cannot bend time or run on empty. How can you help anybody if you do not help yourself? Compassion has to start inside; it has to start with you. If you do not genuinely love and accept yourself how can you really help anyone else?

The word compassion is thrown around freely these days, but it really is more important now than it ever has been. I know time is precious and you may feel like your day is bursting at the seams, with no time for you. Nobody said this would be easy! It is a practice, it takes time, effort, and some cunning tactics if you live in a busy household.

So here are seven steps to reclaiming self-care

Step 1 - The most crucial step in the process! BOUNDARIES. You need to own the word *no*! It is hard, but a hollow yes is no good to anyone. It is half-hearted. Step up and say firmly to your family and friends "I am taking time for myself for the next ...... mins please don't disturb me". If you struggle to escape, the bathroom is a great place to lock yourself in.

Step 2 - Find something that sparks joy in your heart and makes you feel good. It does not need to be complicated; it may be a meditation, affirmations, journaling, yoga or dancing around to your favourite song.

Step 3 - Keep a diary; be accountable to yourself but be kind. I personally use my notes section on my phone.

Step 4 - Cut down the screen time. I know it is hard, it feels like an escape from the hustle and bustle of life. But if you halved your social media time and practised self-care instead, it would not take long for you to feel the benefit.

Step 5 - Check in with your mind and body throughout the day, micro-moments of self-care. While the kettle is boiling, take a couple of deep breaths and scan your body for feelings and sensations. Check in with your mind. Ask yourself, how do I feel physically? How do I feel mentally? Remember, it is ok not to be ok. Knowledge is power when we know how we feel, we can make positive changes.

Step 6 - Stop saying sorry! Instead thank people for respecting your self-care time and your boundaries.

Step 7 - Remember, no matter how hard it is to accept, you cannot change other people's actions, only *your* reaction. You are a human being, be gentle with yourself.

We were not meant to be perfect. Life is full of twists and turns. From time to time it may appear that your path is blocked. But have faith in your mission, in your master plan to find your true north through self-care.

Own your inner Goddess by owning your wellbeing.

How did this chapter make you feel?

Does it change the message because I am a man?
At the start of this chapter, I talked about my preconceived judgments about being a goddess. I now stand tall, knowing that by having faith, and singing my heart's song I can truly become anything I want to be.

My mantra for positive change is cemented in my self-care ritual every day. Mantra for Positive Change Truth Is my True Identity. I bow to my divine wisdom. I remove the darkness from my life to live in the light. I am boundless but live with boundaries. I am limitless and free. I am me.

Find *your* heart song and soar to the stars.

Love & Eternal Light

Scott Hutchison- McDade - Spiritual Teacher

It is time to rise Goddess.

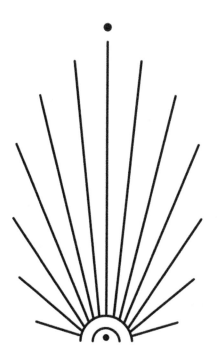

From a very young age I had a sense of things unseen. A sense that there was more, much more. I have been playing with energy since I found my hands. I have always been aware of things beyond the veil, something beyond the illusion of what can and cannot be seen. I am not special. I believe all children can. Children do not hide anything; they are open and receptive. They are honest. Before the age of 7, we are literally like a sponge. We absorb everything from our environment and our experiences. We take everything in, and what we see, and experience becomes our model for the world.

As a child, I talked about the energy I played with and the dreams I had. I knew that I had come here with a purpose. I knew it in my heart, in my soul. I was supposed to be here, and I was supposed to do *something*!

As I grew, I thought I was supposed to change the world. I wanted to change the world, to make it safer, cleaner, fairer for everyone. At that age, I did not understand that the only thing you can change is yourself.

As very small children we live in a bubble of presence. We do not worry about the past, the future or what people think, and I certainly did not. Unfortunately, this does not last, and the world teaches us to be ashamed, to be embarrassed to care what people think. These things are manmade. They are not inherent within us. Remember how carefree you were as a child and how every "don't do that", "don't react like that", "don't behave like this" or "you shouldn't think like that" affected you.

I was a "weird, strange" child. These are not my words, but the words of loved ones, friends, teachers, and people saying it to be cruel. I was often told "You look at things wrong, everyone else sees it like this and you see it like that", or "don't write/draw that, people will think there is something wrong with you. Can't you just be normal!"

Words have power, and what those words teach us is that we have to change.

Perhaps like me, your childhood was spent hiding. Hiding who you were and trying to be who you thought others wanted you to be. As a consequence of trying to watch what I said and did, as a consequence of trying to hide my weirdness, I became very anxious. I suffered mentally and physically and became disconnected from the real world. Living inside my head. I did not make friends easily and I was constantly afraid that people would realise that there was something wrong with me. I developed skin problems, bowel problems and unhealthy addictions. Ultimately, I felt 'wrong', unlovable, and not good enough. Maybe you have experienced something similar.

Through self-development, shadow work and finding my purpose I transformed that awkwardness and fear into my very own super-power.

Nowadays, I shine my weirdness for all to see, wearing it like a super-hero cloak. Unashamedly, unapologetically, weirdly me! I used the words of others and those weird and strange parts of myself to reclaim my power. To realise who I was before they told me who to be. From the ashes of a life I hated, I created a life I love.

As an adult, I realise that those words of my childhood and the pain they caused had created a thought loop in my mind. I was no longer being hurt by others and their words. But I was hurting myself by replaying this negative loop over and over. I was choosing to replay it. I was choosing to live in the pain. I was choosing to be a victim of old words and old pain.

Before I transformed from a victim with a "poor-me" mentality, to a holistic therapist, life was unnecessarily hard. I walked through life like Eeyore, head down, wondering what could go wrong next.

Now, I do not worry what happens. I expect miracles and synchronicities every day. I understand that negative things will happen, but I do not need to be a negative person. I am an incredibly positive person. I love life and bounce from one day to the next. Negative things still happen sometimes, that's life. But I know I can experience pain, anger, frustration and accept it. I know that everything I have experienced and will experience is all making me who I am today and who I will become. I chose this life before I even incarnated into it.

This change did not happen overnight. It took a lot of work. It required me to embrace the pain and upheaval of change. Embrace the emotional and physical pain that comes with transformation. Pain is just a signal that something is not right. Emotional or physical pain is a signal that something needs to change.

Through this transformation I found my power, my calling and my soul's purpose.

Working as a holistic therapist is my purpose. As a child, I thought my purpose was to change the world and of course it is. I came here to transform the world, to help it to move forward into the next evolutionary leap. In the exact same way that you did. All of our purposes are to not change the world but assist in its transformation.

That is why we incarnated into this time and this place. To change the world and help move it onto the next evolutionary stage of development. However, there is a bit of an oxymoron here. You cannot actually change anything but your perception and yourself. The only change you can make is within yourself. You cannot transform the world. You can only transform yourself. The magic is, that in healing yourself, you contribute to healing the planet. By transforming yourself you contribute to the collective transformation of mother earth.

How did I get from where I was to where I am?

How did I go from an unhealed, unhappy person to a badass goddess helping others in their own healing and helping to raise the vibration of the planet?
As Wayne Dyer said,
'I changed the way I looked at things and the things I looked at changed.'

Perception is everything! What you perceive you believe.

I did the work. I ACCEPTED who I was. I took RESPONSIBILITY for where I was, and I took ACTION towards where I wanted to be.

I made a conscious choice to work on myself and my beliefs and change that perception of self; to go into my subconscious, do the necessary shadow work and create new programming and new beliefs. This is where hypnotherapy works wonders.

The work that I have done on self has helped me realise that we help the world heal, by healing ourselves. I am a holistic therapist - a teacher, trainer, coach, and energy healer. Using 'woo-woo' tools such as reiki and seichem alongside more traditional therapies such as hypnotherapy.

Hypnotherapy works on the subconscious, that old, unhelpful programming and literally assists in transforming the way you think, trigger, and respond.

Holistic means working on the whole. Which I believe to be the mind, body, spirit - past, present, future, things seen, things unseen, things intuitively known.

Here are some of the valuable life lessons I learned along the way.
- When you try to please everyone, you please no-one
- When you try to be what you think others want, you lose yourself
- Every time you pretend to agree with something that you really disagree with, your voice gets smaller and smaller, until it disappears
- People respect confidence, people respect boundaries
- Hiding your light causes physical blocks in your energy which can leads to illness

Let me repeat this, loud and clear.

I did not wake up one morning and suddenly: POOF! Instant transformation! Change takes time, dedication, continued awareness, acceptance, and acknowledgement of where you are and what brought you there. It takes commitment to continually take action to get where you want to be.

This is why I became a holistic therapist. This is my purpose. To assist others in transforming their perception and creating a new self-belief.

I assist my clients in remembering who they were before the world told them who to be. To help them accept responsibility for their life, to ensure that they are busy creating a life they love.

In taking responsibility for who they are and where they are in their lives, my clients are able to move from an Eeyore mindset - allowing life to happen to them and just surviving the day, to a thriving Tigger mindset, getting out there and creating a purposeful life for themselves.

You can be a victim of your past or the creator of your present and manifest your future. The choice truly is yours. Whatever has happened to you up to this point, whoever has hurt you. It was not your fault.

BUT

It is your responsibility to heal.

Listen to that again.

It is your responsibility to heal.

One more time.

It is your responsibility to heal.

When I am working with clients, the first thing I tell them is that I am not their healer. As much as my ego would love to lay claim to that. I cannot do that. I came here to heal but I cannot. I cannot heal you and anyone who says that they can are talking rubbish. You are a healer; I am a healer. Every person on this planet is a healer. The catch is that you can only heal yourself. Every tool in my tool kit facilitates and holds the space for you to grow, transform and heal yourself.

Again.

Only you can heal yourself.

One last time

Only you can heal yourself.

All healing is self-healing. People can facilitate, people can hold the space for you. People can hold your hand for parts of the journey. But in the end, the only person who can heal you, is **you**!

The only person who can heal you is you.

Before I started to practice what I preached, I was stuck in a cycle of poor me. Constantly asking myself why was life so hard? Why did everything happen to me?

Once I accepted responsibility for my own healing, once I got out of my head and out of the Universe's way, transformation came. The therapists, the teachers and the mentors came thick and fast.

It is scientifically proven that when we are working towards something good, it has a very positive effect on our lives. We become happier, healthier, more driven. Have you ever noticed that when you are learning a new skill, attending a workshop or group you feel more alive? And in some instances, you can feel your body vibrating? When we feel we are progressing towards something good, we feel fulfilled, happy and that our life has purpose.

It is time to unlearn the things that trigger responses; unlearn self-limiting beliefs; and unlearn outdated and unhelpful programming. It is time to learn self-love, self-compassion, self-belief.

It is time to work towards acceptance, and healing.

Your life does have purpose, you have a purpose. You choose to incarnate into this life, into this time. Right now. Everything in your life that you have experienced has led you to this moment. This moment right now where you are ready. Ready to unleash that inner goddess and take responsibility for who you are.

So, now that you ARE ready what can you do?

Well...

First, you have this book and all the amazing tools from each Goddess. This along with the amazing added value of the free content will set you on your path.

Here is a morning routine to bring acceptance, balance, and a little bit of badassery!

When you wake get yourself in front of a mirror.

Look yourself straight in the eye and say:
> I accept all that I am, and all that I have been
> The good, the bad and the ugly
> I forgive all that I am, all that I have been
> The good, the bad and the ugly
> I celebrate all that I am, and all that I have been
> The good, the bad and the ugly
> I am a Goddess, and I am ready to rise
> I am a Goddess, and I am here
> I am a Goddess, and I am divine
> Today is mine!

Repeat three times!

Then, turn towards where the morning sun would be. Close your eyes and imagine the warm sun on your face and your bare feet on soft dewy grass.

Then say:
> Today is mine, today is mine, today is mine. The Goddess has risen.

Repeat 3 times.

Finish by playing a song which makes you feel amazing. An anthem for your Goddess. If you do not have a song, go find one! It is time to rise Goddess. the earth needs you and all you have to offer!

The time is now!

Lisa Viccars – Holistic Therapist

No is a full sentence.

If I had a penny for every time that I said yes when every atom of my body screamed no, I would be writing this from my private helicopter circling my very own island.

Once I thought that creating my own metaphorical island was the only way in which I could be truly happy. Cut off from the world where I could avoid conflict, this incessant need to people please, and my incredibly frustrating aversion to saying no.

Do you struggle with that little word too?

Old me would lend money while my own bills remained unpaid. Old me would put my commitments and responsibilities aside to ensure that others around me saw to theirs.

Old me would sacrifice time with my family to help others. Old me would sign up for everything. Need a cake baked for some charity event? OK! Need someone to look after your ten children? OK! Want to move in with me rent-free, OK! Need someone to chat to? I will drop everything.

Old me allowed all my important and consequential stuff in my life to be put on the back burner, because everyone knew that they could count on me.

Frustratingly I was every bit as opposed to asking for help as I was saying no.

Does that sound familiar?

It made me feel important and needed. I did not feel comfortable taking up space in people's lives, without offering something in return, to earn it. I felt a need to fix everything for everybody. I was incredibly resentful. I felt everyone was taking advantage of me. I felt personally responsible for every issue I heard about. It destroyed relationships with those around me.

My behaviour led to a cycle of guilt as it affected my presence and financial situation at home.

My answer at the time was to change my phone number frequently, block people, move home. Seriously. For ten years I never stayed in any home longer than 6 months. To escape the rod, I had made for my own back with my avoidance of the word NO.

I felt angry, bitter, frustrated, lonely and powerless. "You are so ******* weak, grow a pair" roared my inner critic.
You may be aware; testicles are pretty fragile. It is not fragility that lies behind this inability to say no. It is evidence of your previous need for strength.

We struggle to say no for various reasons -
- We have been conditioned to believe that saying no is bad, rude even. Consider when you were a child. What would the reaction have been should you have said no to an adult?
- We worry we will let people down, disappoint them.
- We worry we will not meet expectations.
- We worry people will not like/love or accept us.
- We worry people will think we are selfish.
- We have a fear of missing out.
- We fear conflict.
- We feel the need to prove our worth.

Do you relate to anything on this list?

As children we create stories to explain our world. Those stories and beliefs run rampant in our minds, unchecked, until we stop and recognise them for what they truly are. That they are not necessarily fact, but rather our own unique interpretation.

We all have a unique perspective of the world; children tend to personalise their negative interactions. As a child, the adults in our life appear godly to us. We rely on them to teach us. If they get something wrong, we do not blame them.

We make it something about us. Children perceive themselves to be to blame in situations where an adult would be able to take all things into consideration.

People generally assume they have a good sense of self-worth. Often because they do not consider their past experiences to be traumatic. But the subconscious beliefs that you are not good enough, do not know enough, are not as worthy as, can stem from various experiences. These common core beliefs hold many back from their personal growth.

During my training, I coached a gentleman whose sister had been unwell throughout their childhood. His mother's time and attention were focused on the care of his brother. He created a belief that his needs were less important than others.

From overly critical parents to bullying to abuse. Many experiences can spark off this train of thought.

As adults we can look at these situations from a different angle and see how mistaken we were. Until we address and identify our beliefs, they run the show behind the scenes.

When we do not feel worthy or good enough, we look for validation externally. We base what we feel about ourselves on what we believe others think of us.

Looking again at the list of reasons why we struggle to say no. Can you see the connection?

Do you feel 'good enough?'

Becoming confident enough to say no, completely transformed my life.

You got this!

Some things you need to learn:

You will never be able to please everyone.
Once you begin to understand the complexities behind your own thoughts, values, and beliefs, you will start to appreciate how unique we all are. Trying to be everything to everyone will lead you further from yourself and probably make you as miserable and disconnected as it did me.

Are you experiencing this?

No-one is going to pop up one day with a medal and congratulate you because you have been deemed worthy.
There is no checklist to tick off. It is for you to take ownership of. A decision you must make followed by small but mighty steps to your destination.
Are you ready to decide that you are worthy?

Your boundaries will trigger some people.
This is a clear sign they are needed. Not everyone sets out to take advantage of you. It can feel that way but there may be some good eggs in your circle. They will respect your boundaries even if the change does come as a shock.

Placing boundaries where previously there were none will change the dynamics of your relationships. Some people will respect your boundaries and your reasons for having them.

There will be others who get mad. For example, you never say no to a friend or family member because you are fearful of conflict. You may relate it to rejection, fearful that if you say no, they will dislike you, or may abandon or reject you.

You have always said yes, when it was not right for you, when you have not wanted to. One day you decide to honour *your* wants and needs, create a boundary, and say no.

The other person gets mad. They are used to you being a pleaser and have previously taken advantage of your lack of boundaries. They may argue, guilt trip, get upset. You saying no reflects unhealed wounds of their own and shines a spotlight on their sense of self-worth. They may feel rejected and abandoned or associate it with their own lack of worth. Some people seek validation by controlling others.

If someone gets mad with a boundary you put in place, it is a clear sign that it was needed. They are not being respectful of you or your needs.

You can see how other people's response to your boundaries has little to do with you. It is more about what is going on in their thought process. You are not to blame, try not to take responsibility for that.

Conflict is scary. But when you begin work on your self-worth you will appreciate that you are as valuable as anyone else. You will become more confident in asserting yourself. Conflict comes down to an expectation going un-met. If someone expects you to behave as you always have and say yes, they may be disappointed when you say no. Only you can decide what to do if someone crosses your boundaries and does not respect you. We often associate what we do and who we are with our worthiness. What we give to the world. Do you make the same association?

Consider a new-born baby. In that vein of thought, that baby is worthless. Do you believe that to be true?

You are worthy by just being.

You are not here to fulfil other people's purpose.

That concept can feel unnatural. Like a pair of new shoes, uncomfortable and a little painful at first. But in time they feel like a second layer of skin. I would be lying if I told you I never feel unworthy now and then. Even writing this chapter, I hear a little voice saying, "you are not good enough to be here". You are reading this! I have obviously given it the finger. Once you are aware of that voice you become adept at calling out your own nonsense. Give yourself time.

Learning to say no was scary, but I picked up some tips along the way.

Build tolerance for that uncomfortable anxiety you feel in that situation.
Start with people whose relationship you are confident will withstand your new boundaries. That will mean different things to different people. Consider who or in what situation you could begin saying no. For me it was at work, every day I was asked to either work through my break, stay late, or take on responsibilities not my own. I said yes out of fear for my future prospects. I was incredibly anxious however I felt powerful and confident. Each time I said no it became a little more natural.

Resist the urge to say yes immediately.

I had become so used to saying yes that I had stopped even considering an alternative. My new auto-response "Let me get back to you on that." The magic words that would just allow me a moment to consider whether I could muster the courage to say no.

Ask yourself, what do I want to do? Am I doing it for the right reasons? Does it come at a cost to you that you will resent? If you are saying yes out of fear, explore what is behind that fear. It is important to acknowledge when we are creating a monster in our heads. Beware of going down the 'what if' rabbit hole and coming up with the worst possible outcome you can think of.

I have come to realise that all of my worst-case scenarios revolve around fear of my unworthiness being confirmed. I will not get the promotion; my partner will leave me; my friend will never speak to me again; I will be destitute. Now I remind myself that that thought process is outdated.

I am worthy.

No relationship I ever have, no situation that I want to be in will ever require me to betray or abandon myself.

You, your highest worthy self, in all of your goddess power. I have found myself in situations where I wanted to say yes but it caused me difficulty. It was a revelation that I could say yes, or I could place that decision in the hands of the other person.

I owned a day spa for a time. Running a business brings its own difficulties for someone who struggles to say no. I frequently worked unreasonable hours to accommodate everyone. The first time that I told a client that we could accommodate her group booking out of hours, but their session would be shorter to ensure staff got their well-deserved time off, it blew my mind. Your 'yes' can suit you.

I have learned that most people are fine with a no, they like to know where they stand. Do not be tempted to soften the blow with "let me see what I can do" or "I will try my best" when you have no intention of doing so. It is unfair to them and stressful for you. You will not feel good about it.

Saying no is not selfish. Putting yourself first is not selfish. Remember, "you can't pour out of an empty cup" and "put on your own oxygen mask first". We have all been there. Physically, mentally, and emotionally drained, struggling to keep our heads above water.

You deserve more than that. Treat yourself as you would someone you love.

Lying is just stressful. Once upon a time, I made up an elaborate lie about my whereabouts to avoid visiting someone.

Unbelievably, the queen visited the same place during my visit and there were cameras everywhere. I was so stressed and paranoid about being caught out, I spent the entire trip dodging cameras and looking over my shoulder and not really enjoying it. All to avoid simply telling my family that I could not visit on that occasion due to very limited time. Because I feared offending them. From that experience I learned that most people would be more upset by a lie, than an honest no.

It is important to recognise when your help is not helpful. I had a friend with an incredibly poor relationship with money. She would frequently run out. If it came to her and her children needing something, I would step in. My continual help hindered her. She never learned to manage her money better. I was enabling her behaviour.

A client of mine had a friend in a poor relationship. She was drained by the constant support she offered. When she withdrew a little it allowed her friend the space to reach into her own strength and find her own answers.

You do not need to justify yourself or explain why you cannot help.

When it comes to saying no confidently, be honest, precise, nice, and true to yourself.

Remember your worth.

Remember that you are a goddess.

Amy Whistance – Holistic Therapist

Trauma is your journey to a beautiful awakening.

What is this journey of Awakening, and how do we fully get in touch with our Inner Goddess? Having been on my Spiritual Path for about 20 years I am very grateful to be where I am now.

Before I found my Inner Goddess, I always felt like I did not fit in. I was sensitive to other people's moods, and actions. I took everything personally. I found myself in relationships where I was taken advantage of and gave too much only to be hurt in the end. I would "cycle" through relationships.

At first, we would get along great. But I always started to feel how different I was, and I would separate myself. I did not want superficial conversations. I wanted to talk about angels, guides, intuition, love, and Universal Laws. I had opened my Reiki business, excited to share my gifts with the world! But instead, I was criticized and misunderstood. I felt lonely, out of place and, frankly, weird.

During that time, I was also married to a narcissist for many years. I did not realize it until years later. You know the type. They put you on a pedestal only to slowly tear you down, and you lose all concept of identity and personal power. I eventually stopped living my truth because I did not know what that was. I lost my voice because I did not speak up or stand up for myself. I began to lose faith with my connection to Source. I lost faith in my own Being. My only saving grace was being Mom to my two beautiful children. Only to lose my boy in a car accident a few years later.

And with that, I tumbled down further into the black hole.

There have been a few turbulent years since then, but I am very grateful to be LIVING my Goddess truth! I have shed all unhealthy relationships from my life. Yes! All of them! I have created beautiful boundaries. I have a loving, caring man that I love to the moon and back. I have close, personal relationships with a small circle of friends that I love and trust. I have expanded my "spiritual circle" to include a community of like-minded, soul based, loving women. And a few men!

Life is like a breath of fresh air to me now. I live from a space of love. I choose to see the love and light within each being, and within myself. Some days are still difficult around grief, and I definitely have my triggers. I identify them, give them grace, and work through them. I am patient with myself and allow myself the "down days" when I need them. I turn to daily meditation for calm and clarity. I dive into nature to ground and feel connected to the beauty and strength of Gaia. And with the support of so many loving friends and family around me, I have reestablished my energy healing and coaching business.

This time, I am confident in my gifts, and what I have to offer the world!

The journey to get here has been quite a ride. I learned from a few more narcissists that I really did not need or want that type of relationship in my life. Live and learn, and now I am passing on wisdom to others who are recovering from narcissistic relationships and emotional abuse.

The key is recognizing the red flag behaviors. For example, playing the victim, gaslighting, and lying, to name just a few. And when you begin moving on, learning when NOT to react. A narcissist feeds off of your reaction. You can stop them dead in their tracks when you do not respond. And in not responding, you begin to recognize your own strength. And there is the magic! Your Goddess has just stepped in.

When I lost my boy, I went to a place I never knew existed, somewhere no mother should ever have to go. But because of my understanding of how Spirit works, and my relationship with Source, I was able to come to terms with my loss. My boy had a much bigger purpose than this human experience. He is my angel, and an angel to so many more. He visits now and then and I am so grateful. In conversations with him, he has told me, "Mom, you will be speaking about this one day, and helping lots of other Moms along the way."

I have drawn inspiration from him and also a very special partnership with my energy healer, Akayah Blake. We worked together to release my boy from his belief that it was his responsibility to stay here, to take care of me and his sister. It was a beautiful send off to the light and his bigger purpose.

Grief is a very personal journey. There is no "right way" or "wrong way", only your way. There is definitely shock at first. And that can last a long time. Sadness, depression, anger, guilt; all happen in their own time. The best way to live with grief is with grace. Give yourself the grace to be sad or depressed. It may last for a moment or for days at a time.

Give yourself the grace to feel joy. It is normal to feel guilty being happy, because maybe you should always feel sad. But remember that joy exists within us, always. It is meant to and it is OK to feel it. I feel my boy is happy for me, happy that I live life in joy! High five Buddy!

You could say I have experienced trauma over the years. But I do not identify as those traumas. They are experiences that have led me to live my most Goddess-powered life imaginable. To recover from these experiences took strength, insight, and learning from other spiritual communities.

One that I have tapped into the last couple of years is John Burgos' Beyond the Ordinary Show. It is a webinar that hosts Spiritual mentors, intuitives, visionaries and channelers, etc. They share the same wisdom that we are ALL Source Light, we are all One, we are all Love. They encourage us to live in our power, and that we are all Pure Potential.

We create our realities through our thoughts, intentions, and bold actions. And when we face big or small roadblocks in life, we ask "How is this happening FOR me, not TO me?" The Universe is always conspiring for our absolute best.

The journey of Awakening is personal and yet Universal. It contains both hardships and wins. But it is a journey that you will always cherish. No matter where you are in your journey, you always have your inner Goddess with you. She exists and has always existed. If you have been through a traumatic experience, be it in a relationship or the loss of a loved one, I invite you to seek Freedom. By Freedom, I mean declaring that the trauma no longer holds power over you. You are no longer a victim, but a survivor and a Goddess. All the love, light, power, and strength to live the life of magic and Joy you deserve is within you.

Please take a few moments and write down your thoughts around these questions.

- If you were able to heal from the trauma and triggers, what new outlook would you have on life?

- If you were able to break through the limited beliefs you have created for yourself (IE, I am not good enough), what new possibilities do you see for your life?

- If you were to find your voice and purpose, what impact could you make on others?

My wish is to reach thousands of women around the world with this message. Our journey to awakening, as beautiful as it is, can also be filled with traumatic experiences or toxic relationships. We can heal from these with the knowledge that we ARE Source Light. Our Inner Goddess already exists! Tapping into that gives us the strength to heal and keep moving forward on our journey. We are no longer victims. We are good enough. And we deserve to live our most Goddess Empowered life!

Love and Light my fellow Goddesses!

Randi Willhite – Biofeedback Spiritual Coach

Uncover the emotional energy behind your experience.

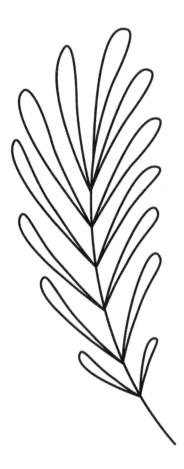

"Keep going," I said, bursting into tears, ignoring the warning signs, waving him on in embarrassment. My explosion of emotion then manifested into hiccups, streams of tears, and bubbling snot. "Just ignore it," I told him.

My dad was trying to have a conversation with me, and I felt I was losing a battle. Defeated, I pushed my emotions back inside, adding to my list of limiting beliefs. *What is the use in expressing myself? I won't be heard anyway.*

Grim thoughts for a kid, I suppose. However, if I look back at my childhood, my emotional battle was not with him, or anyone else, but with myself, and all the emotional energy I suspected was hidden within me. Later I would learn how true that suspicion was.

With that teary outburst, any attempt to control my emotional response failed. The tears came as a sign of much needed relief. Back then, I did not have the emotional tools or maturity to get to the root of my problems, so my emotions remained trapped inside until extreme discomfort of my physical body got my attention enough to do something about it. I wish I had known the consequences of suppressing emotions back then.

The Burden of Stuck Emotions on The Physical Body
Next, in my mid-twenties, I experienced a full on, cannot breathe, emotional and physical breakdown at work. They called the paramedics. I failed to hold back waves of shame and vulnerability while trying to calm down.

"Breathe," the paramedic told me. Lost in emotional and physical pain, I was barely conscious of what I was doing. My body knew otherwise, though. In that moment, my body could only play out what was escaping from inside my energy field. Something had to give, and it did- my body, my job, and my drive to do it all myself.

The Ancestral Legacy of Stuck Emotional Energy
After several years of dealing with severe brain fog, fatigue, and despair, I connected with several incredible health care professionals, chiropractor, naturopathic doctor, and acupuncturist included, who supported me in coaxing back my physical health. But after a few more years, my progress hit a wall.

Witnessing my struggle, my mom introduced me to a book called the *Emotion Code®* by Dr. Bradley Nelson. Seeing that I was open to the idea, she offered to demonstrate releasing trapped emotions from me.

She had only released a couple of emotions when I noticed a difference. It dawned on me that perhaps the solution I was seeking was not physical at all; it was energetic. Emotions were energetic. Perhaps those moments of misery I had lived through, extreme and as uncomfortable as they were, served a purpose. In fact, I was much more motivated and open to what I might not have considered before. I wanted a solution badly.

Though I was skeptical, unsure if energy healing would really work, I was desperate. In fact, I got certified in several healing modalities, just to understand them more and to find solutions to my physical and emotional challenges.

After working on myself, then some clients for a while, I started to notice some fascinating patterns. For instance, a woman in her 40s or 50s came to me with some "hip stuff." I did not ask for details. We did a session, and I released 11 trapped emotions from her. Intriguingly, all but two of them were from one to three generations back on both sides of her family. I did not think much of it until she contacted me a week later.

"Jena, I waited to see if the pain was gone or if it would come back," she explained. "It's gone!" Apparently, several female members of her family had already undergone hip replacements, and even the physical or massage therapist she had worked with thought, *there is something stuck.*

Wow, I thought. Trauma energy really can get passed down and affect the entire family, **as if it gets stuck in the DNA, in cellular memory.**

After looking closer at emotions released and positive outcomes achieved by others and myself, I noticed more though-provoking patterns. These emotional energies being released were *ancient*. Thousands of years ancient. Soul ancient. I discovered that the most common ancient, trapped emotions were abandonment, despair, and anxiety. Worry, discouragement, frustration, and bitterness were not far behind. This realization set me on another personal healing track. **I decided** that if I wanted to feel more empowered and more myself, my true self, I needed to shed as much ancient, ancestral, and personal emotional baggage as possible.

It took me years to understand the connection between emotions and energy. We are not taught this kind of stuff. Perhaps we should be.

From Energy Burdened to Energy Empowered

Though I had shunned them previously, I began using oracle cards to explore what was coming up in my energy field because it finally hit me that that my energy and emotions would always reveal through the cards what I needed to hear most.

I started to observe a pattern in the cards, just like the trapped energies I had previously released. I kept pulling cards related to ancestor healing, and I noticed myself being drawn to seminars and talks about generational and ancestral healing.

I kept feeling extreme discomfort in my body and felt the need to clear more ancestral energy from my field, though I had no conscious idea of how to do it.

So, I pooled my energetic and healing resources together and embarked on a year-long healing journey using my skills as an Angelic Reiki™ practitioner and Master Teacher to do an intentional daily session on myself based on my discomforts and my heart-felt desires. I committed to writing my intentions down before each session, what I noticed during, and a few oracle card messages after to chronicle where my energy was heading.

On the seventh day into my healing adventure, I wrote down eleven intentions, some to do with personal power and ancestral healing, and the most intense and extraordinary things happened. I sat in sacred space with my beautiful Angelite stones and felt a strong and loving healing presence. Then I felt a bit of midsection pain on the left side of my body as if an energetic knife were being pulled from me. After, I felt a freedom and security I had not felt for years.

Energy streamed into each of my palms at the end of my healing as if to get me to *consciously* notice the power and energy there. It was literally in my own hands. My hands were an extension of my heart. My heart connected to source energy, or the Divine, or God. My power flowed from this divine source and when it did, I was in perfect divine balance. The peace and self-awareness I felt after that was profound. To top it off, the next-step card I pulled after the session was all about answering the call of my soul.

Six months later, I sang my first heart-felt, intuitive, soul guided, self-expressing intention into being, and I have not stopped since. The young adult who suppressed her emotions and voice to the point of uncontrollable tears has transformed into a super-powered goddess who guides people to remember their infinite potential and ability within their human selves.

I *love* what I do now as an energy healer and teacher. When I work, I feel on top of the world, excited to get going, creating through song. I have stepped into my goddess super-power, the power that was there all along. I just needed some energetic cleansing to remember.

I am often reminded of how fortunate and grateful I am for clearing away my own emotional baggage. Having this mode of expression and means to help others is vital to me now. It is what I feel I was born to do. If I had not been so determined to find a state of inner calm and healing, I would never have discovered this amazing gift.

Some goddesses discover their superpowers at a young age and spend many years coming to terms with them before they radiate their empowered selves. Other goddesses spend years clearing the trauma surrounding theirs and activate them later. Each path serves.

Feeling despair or not good enough can keep these superpowers hidden, though. Getting schooled by emotions, emotional habits and patterns can feel overwhelming. But this is the exact moment to summon gratitude from the depths of the soul for this training because while it may be the most gut-wrenching, bone fatiguing, life whirling thing to experience, it could also be the most soul satisfying and powerful.

That being said, if you have not discovered your goddess superpower yet, do not take it to heart. To become an emotional master, one must train. Here is a training framework that I have used to help me access my goddess power.

The first step requires noticing what emotions come up with a bit of detachment. Once the noticing has occurred, the active training can begin!

The training is to move toward emotions that bring joy and away from emotions that sabotage us and keep us in low vibrating states. This can be accomplished through activities that feel good. Perhaps that is yoga, painting, meditating, running, therapy, energy healing sessions or education of some sort. In my case, it is doing energetic healing, especially through song.

When we discover what gets us shining, we can start choosing more of that. Alternatively, we can feel this inner light without having the external results yet intensifying the feeling within our hearts to invite it into our lives.

Finally, we can witness the power coming to life. How this shows up may be completely unexpected. I had no idea it would come in the form of soul-remembering sound transmissions.

I have come to see that the heart transmits our intentions into our environment, like a signature vibration. Emotions that are trapped within contribute to and change what that signature vibration is like. Stuck emotions can obscure the windows of our hearts. Even if we want to transmit love, we may not be able to because of clouded windows. By cleaning up our inner world, we can access the power of our hearts to radiate a clearer vibration out into our environments. This is where our power comes from.

Your power is as strong as your energy field.

If you get stuck, you may realize, as I did, that you cannot do it all on your own, and that painful surrender is actually a blessing in disguise. As you emerge from your solitary struggle, pushing past the worry of what people may think of you, pushing past the unconscious self-battering, opening up with the determination to heal, to move beyond, you allow that small opening of opportunity in.

Then we can set off a chain reaction in our energy fields and the environment around us. We start to come into our power.

So, have you given yourself permission to be healed and to step into your Goddess power, or do you suspect you are still running old emotional programming?

When you notice and acknowledge uncomfortable emotions, then you can make the choice to let them be a foothold in your life or not. Knowing how is not necessary in the beginning, but the willingness and declaration of intent is crucial; it is the permission. It is the catalyst, the spark.

For me, emotional mastery is not about controlling all the subconscious and conscious emotions; it is about owning our power and responsibility to clear out the emotional baggage keeping us stuck in old emotional patterns whether they are ancient or not, personal, or not.

Begin to clear out that baggage and we can strengthen our inner emotional platforms. Here are five tips I would love to share for emotional platform strengthening.

- Build a daily practice of energy & emotional state scanning. Write what you feel on small sticky notes. Fix them to a wall or in a journal & take a look at the patterns on a weekly or monthly basis. Then choose the new pattern you would like to create instead.
- Get acquainted with a guidance or oracle deck to have perspective on your current energetic or emotional state so you can shift it.
- Choose to enact stronger energetic boundaries. Instead of allowing people to vent their emotions, try saying this: "I hear you. What would you *love* to experience instead?" They may be shocked into silence, or they may play along. Experience the shift in energy.

- Take a workshop or a class from a teacher you resonate with to empower and educate yourself about working with the emotional and energetic environment around you.
- When you try your best and still cannot seem to connect with your heart-felt desires and goals, seek out some assistance. Recognize when the best self-care you can give yourself is having someone hold a safe space for you to heal.

From this inner platform that you have strengthened, you may notice yourself reacting to situations, circumstances, and people around you from that state of inner power. You can begin to create what your soul desires from that state of inner power. That power is your everyday goddess power.

Jena Robinson – Energy Healer

When the Goddess is muted.

"Where are you?" said the stern voice on the other end of the phone line.

"I am coming home right away." She replied, in a trembling voice.

Dumping everything she had grabbed to buy, she ran towards the car park and headed straight home.

Back then, she would have struggled to find the courage to ask if it were urgent for her to rush home, or to confidently assert that she would be home after she had finished her shopping.

Professionally, she had a great job. She worked hard to please her bosses and do as she was told, without question. She could not speak up for herself even though deep within she longed to be heard. But whenever she tried to speak, the FEAR would grip her so tightly that it hurt her bones. She felt as though she was buried in a box with such steep sides, she saw no point in trying to climb out. Feeling suffocated she moved mechanically through the days like a zombie, while pretending to the world that she was happy, confident, and lucky.

Does this all sound familiar?

I can relate to how she felt as this is my story. Chasing validation, approval, and love from other people, I would only say what I thought people wanted to hear, what would please them. That was what I had learnt in my childhood. "Speak to please". I learned to hide my emotions, and my true feelings so that I would blend in. I did not want to stand out, be rejected, mocked, or even worse, be murdered for speaking my mind. That is an exaggeration, but the greatest fear we all have.

I accepted fear as part of my life. Allowed it to stop me from speaking up, to keep me safe. FEAR reminded me of past painful experiences when I was mocked, rejected, or judged for exposing my true emotions. I guess I developed strategies to hide my deeper feelings, my authentic self.

Cultural conditioning and growing up in a dysfunctional family led me to believe:

- My needs are not important, and I do not need to speak up.
- Expressing my needs is selfish.
- I need love from my caretakers in order to survive and I need to do whatever is required of me to get it.
- I am valued and needed when I am speaking to please others.
- My opinion does not matter, and I do not matter.
- I am weird. There is something wrong with me and in order to feel validated I need to blend in. I do that by saying what others want to hear.
- People might think I am crazy if I reveal my true feelings, so it is better to keep my thoughts to myself.
- As the family peacekeeper it is my job to sacrifice my own needs to keep the peace.
  And many more

All these beliefs led to me to masking my personality, spending my life pleasing others in the hope of being approved, validated and above all loved.

"When you are born to stand out, you can't blend in"
-Wonder Movie

Life began showing me signs that something needed to change. But I chose to be oblivious to those signs and continued snubbing and criticising myself until I was exhausted.

I turned to God, as I could not find answers on my own. After 6 months of continuous meditation, I heard an echoing voice in my head: "Aren't you tired yet? Would you like to experience joy?". "Yes" jumped out my mouth. And I heard, "Find your voice, know thyself."

I was startled and confused. "Find my voice, know myself? Surely these are my thoughts speaking", I scoffed. I chose to ignore what I had heard and continued focusing on the hustle and bustle of my life. But the Universe continued speaking to me in mysterious ways.

My relationships with other people began to deteriorate. So, I became an automaton, going through the motions to please others and keep the peace. But this time it was different. The voices became louder and my feelings of suffocation strangled my heart.

Life seemed determined to inflict pain until I surrendered and started to listen.

As I continued to meditate, divine support and guidance helped me move forward, one step at a time. My old habits no longer resonated with me. I turned to my energy healing for help, as I understood that I could not make these changes with just my intellectual mind. Healing helped me re-establish the connection with my long forgotten inner child who was waiting for help.

It was as though I had been unplugged from a life of sleepwalking and shown the way to heal myself.

The inner work was not easy, but I began to honour my needs, connect to my true self, and listen to my inner VOICE. The more I worked on myself, the stronger I felt.

After decades of hiding, I found a way to speak out, to reveal myself. I began to avoid situations where I before I would cower. With weeks of relentless practice, I framed how to communicate my emotional needs in the most loving way to my closest relation. Difficult at first, it was surprising how easily I felt fulfilled by speaking from my heart in a loving way and putting boundaries in place.

But it began creating cracks in my 15-year marriage, as the girl once content to sit in the shadows evolved. People gave free advice on what I should or should not do, judged me as unstable, or someone with mental issues. But the whisper of "WISP of WINGS" was loud enough to clear my confusion, by showing what was right for me. Standing up for myself, facing the fear with courage, helped me honour myself and my inner desires. I shrugged off the restraints that I had allowed others to place upon me, allowing me to feel LIMITLESS.

People were disappointed with me as I was changing, and I no longer fit into their idea of how I should be. But one step at a time, I continued on, despite the critic in my mind howling, "Are you crazy? STOP! Turn back."

I had triggered a chain reaction which led to a shocking experience that broke down everything I was attached to. It was frightening and terrifying, to stand in my power alone particularly when my cultural background had taught me to suppress my feelings, to oblige others, especially after marriage. To keep the peace. I was conditioned to believe that a woman needs to sacrifice, endure any behaviour, for the sake of family.

The slow death of my own self had far greater consequences than losing someone I loved, someone I was attached to.

> *"You can have anything you want if you want desperately enough.*
> *You must want it with an exuberance that erupts through the skin*
> *and joins the energy that created the world"*
> *-Sheila Graham*

My life-changing moment came, when I looked into the eye of the fear and said, "BRING IT ON." Though I knew it would shake my roots if I went against what I had been taught to do, I kept marching on because I was sick of being sick and tired, and I wanted CHANGE.

> *"How can you hesitate? Risk! Risk anything!*
> *Care no more for others' opinions, for those voices. Face the truth"*
> *- Katherine Mansfield*

I embraced the suffering because I wanted the absolute freedom to speak my truth even when it meant losing so much. I chose the unknown over fear, and that opened the gateway to my heart. My life fell apart and the person I was disappeared for good. There was no turning back from this journey.

It is said, "*The only way through is to go through.*" Sometimes, I felt like I was tied to a spinning wheel which was spewing out the baggage that I no longer needed. I found myself in a no man's land for a long time, as I could not relate to who I used to be and yet the new 'Me' was not ready. I felt anger, pain, resentment, guilt, shame, and every emotion that had been long buried.

I accepted and acknowledged the darker side of me, my emotions, and undermining patterns of behaviour, without self-judgement or criticism. Unravelled the conditioning and experiences behind each part, releasing that which no longer served me, with love to transmute in Divine Light. My inner VOICE nudged me, pushed me to where I am now, feeling free and authentic.

With this healing came:

- Realisation of self-worth. I am born worthy and I do not need to oblige other's wishes to feel my worth.
- Knowing that my voice matters, I will speak up for myself no matter how hard it seems.
- I will choose Truth over Fear. I will choose love for myself over FEAR.
- Recognition of my Inner strength and power. I can step into my power with bravery and courage.
- I do not need external validation in order to feel loved, I turn to inner validation instead.
- No one can or will speak for me. Only I know how I feel. What others say about me is their projection.

If someone asks me, "Was it easy?" I say "NO, NOT AT ALL"
And if they ask, "Was that worth it?", I say "YES, ABSOLUTELY"

Our voice is never lost. It is always inside of us. Sometimes we cannot hear it because we are tuned to a different frequency. One of shame, guilt, anger, jealousy, or resentment. We reveal our voice by connecting to our inner self. We make that connection by peeling off the layers between our outer world and inner world. There is no magic pill to help us heal quickly. It requires inner work.

What is this inner work? How do I begin? If you are willing to step in and take a leap into the unknown, then you have already taken the first step towards feeling alive and exuberant.

- Sit in SILENCE to hear the storm. Even for just 5 minutes a day. As you spend more time with yourself alone, you create a relationship with your own self, your intuition, soul self or inner child.
- Become AWARE of what you are feeling. Negative emotions, repeating patterns of behaviour or things that trigger you. Do not run away from the feeling. The more you shove under the rug, the bigger the pile gets and ultimately life will throw experiences at you to wake you up.
- Know that it is ok to feel the way you are feeling - because none of us have been taught to deal with our emotions. We have been asked to control them, I never understood how. How to control something which is boiling like a volcano inside. Brushing it off or being told, "You are weird to feel the way you are feeling." These experiences form the damaged psychology which leads us to use defensive mechanisms to protect us by repression, displacement, reaction formation, Introjection, projection etc.

- Ask yourself these questions to help reveal your fears and the thoughts which hold you back from speaking up:
    - What are you scared might happen, if you reveal your true self and speak out: Abuse, losing your relationships, being mocked, losing your job?
    - Do you often discourage yourself from speaking up feeling it is dumb?
    - Do you fear disappointing people around you by saying, doing, eating, or wearing what you want?
    - Do you feel you are not good enough or smart enough to pitch in?

- ACCEPT everything about yourself. Every part, bare, raw, and naked, however hard it seems. Do this with the COMPASSION, KINDNESS and LOVE we freely give to others. And above all no judgement.

I wrote a poem for my inner child:

> *"Let that girl within be FREE,*
> *Let her know the love,*
> *Let her wings flutter,*
> *Let that whisper caress,*
> *Let her be,*
> *And there she roars high,*
> *Judge her not and let her breathe,*
> *Set her free, free, free"*

- BE KIND to yourself: No matter what you do, no matter how hard the situation is, or what mistakes you make. Do nothing that makes you feel uncomfortable. Treat yourself with the compassion you would show your own child. It can be scary and almost impossible to grasp the concept of your inner child. It was for me. But with a little help I connected to that little girl within me.

- Instead of saying, "You idiot, dumb, stupid girl, you did it again." Say "I know it is hard to change old habits but Hey! Look! at least you noticed! That's great!" Learn to honour yourself by saying, "I am sorry that I have been treating you this way all the time, I ask for your forgiveness". Forgiveness brings empowerment and strength.

- Find your TRIGGERS. With proper guidance and support, you can deal with them, and heal your emotional bruises and wounded parts by integrating the fragments lost to become whole in yourself.
Then you can step into your true self and connect to that VOICE, which brings Clarity, Certainty, Confidence, Freedom and Strength. This voice surpasses everything else that no longer needs external validation. And there you will be - speaking your authentic self.

There are no easy solutions to healing, but by showing patience, compassion, resilience and above all LOVE for ourselves we can savour the journey in the moment and worry less about the destination.

I will end with a quote inspired by Charles Blondin's story that helped me during the tough time:

"Belief makes it possible,
Faith makes it real,
And TRUST makes it easier"

Wishing you love and all the great things!!

Shveta S – Intuitive Therapist

Connecting to your purpose, the brave way.

There is a lot that I remember about the day that changed my life.

Walking through one of the most desired neighborhoods in South Tampa, I recall the vibrant colors of the trees, the outlines of massive houses with endless manicured lawns and my sons skipping ahead of me on our short walk to their school.

The bitter argument with my narcissist the night before had left a toxic residue flowing through my body, like the blood in my veins. The pleasant smile fixed on my face, as I waved to neighbors and chatted with fellow PTA Board members, barely disguised the tension I held inside me, a depleted shell of the woman I once was.

Stepping back inside my home, tears streamed down my face as the weight of "faking it" bore down on me like a ton of bricks. My chest constricted and I sobbed, walking down the hallway to my bedroom. Feeling like I was about to implode, my vision blurred, and I crumpled onto my bed.

I remember feeling an energy surge through my body as I threw myself around the bed, crying out to God, full of pain, frustration, and shame. Punching the bed and screaming out, "WHY??!! I can't do this anymore!". I rolled out of the bed onto my knees and just cried thinking, "I don't even know what I need right now but God has to know that this is too much! I cannot keep living in shame and embarrassment. Suffering in silence, finding myself in yet another relationship where I love someone so much, but they treat me like their number one enemy."

I cried until there were no tears left. But then I remember a distinct stillness coming over me. As I lay back in my bed and stared at the ceiling, I heard my inner voice saying, "Now what are you going to do about it?", and I realized that tears were not going to help me get back to the woman I was before the narcissist. The woman that believed in dreams and loved herself, imperfect as she was. Who felt genuinely happy and blessed most of the time. Who once viewed life as vibrant, full of wonder and beautiful expectations.

I also heard, "This isn't what I planned for your life! You are in this situation because you don't believe that you deserve better anymore"

For years I had immersed myself in metaphysical books about manifestation and co-creation, back in a time when I felt connected to God and the Source of dreams fulfilled. But after meeting my first narcissist that changed.

While he set about building me up to feel like the greatest woman on earth, I unwittingly made him "God". When he brought me down with physical, verbal, and mental abuse, I no longer believed in myself or anything else. I no longer trusted myself because how could I fall in love with someone so venomous, so ugly?

One of my team members said to me, "Narcissists don't break into poor houses. They break into mansions." I never saw the deliberate steps each narcissist I was with took to break down my confidence, destroy my purpose and remove my connection to others.

All I knew was that while I was in back-to-back relationships with narcissists, I went from being top of the leaderboard in business, in my community and life in general, to rock bottom. I was in a constant state of confusion, wondering how the hell did I end up here?!

I had been a successful, confident leader who knew about the power of prayer and the laws of attraction. So how the fuck did I end up at this point? Where I reached for makeup, to cover the bruises on my neck, before going to dinner with the "love of my life". Where I walked on eggshells in my own home, trying to create a healthy environment for my babies and not spark the rage which would trigger yet another never-ending argument over complete bullshit.

On that beautiful day when I entered the dark night of my soul, I reached for my Bible. If I was hearing that voice in my head saying I'm settling, then what are these promises God spoke about? I googled God's promises, looked up the corresponding scriptures. I researched sermons to see what I was missing, and I found scripture after scripture, line after line, screaming out about God promising to fulfill my dreams, deliver abundant gifts, more than I could ever imagine.

I became determined to hold God to these promises. I wanted a life better than the one I was experiencing because I realized that if I kept going, kept suffering in silence, too embarrassed to talk to those I loved about my situation because I was still in it, I would have nothing left to give my babies, my business, or myself. I could not take the emotional drain any longer and I was sick of faking It.

I had tried to put together a "plan" to leave before. But I started to see that I had created my adult identity around the wealthy lifestyle I experienced with my narcissists, so different to that of my childhood and I was trying to find a way to leave while still maintaining that lifestyle. And although I had built a successful business up to almost $750k in only 8 months, I was unable to put a deposit down on a place for my sons and I because my partner controlled the finances.

That night I called my girlfriend and asked if I could crash on her couch for an undetermined amount of time with my two sons. She welcomed us with open arms and that changed my life. We had a month-long sleepover full of love, with no judgment. Sleeping on that couch with my babies on an air mattress in her living room allowed me to feel genuine happiness again.

During that time, I realized that the thing that I did not want to do the most, was the thing I needed the most. The time away from my narcissist allowed me to nurture my new fierce determination to do more. Want more. To dream big again and use my experiences to my benefit in some way.

The idea of stepping into something better on the other side of narcissism gave me hope, but boy oh boy was I scared! I rationalized in my mind how I could stay and make it work. Maybe they would wake up and realize what they had in front of them. See that I only wanted to love them, that I would always see them at their best even though they kept showing me their worst. The weight on me had lifted while staying with my friend so I talked myself into going back, with the idea of making a "plan" to leave. Ironically, this delayed me leaving because I was too scared!

The confidence I once felt was overshadowed by all of the lies that my partner told me about myself. I wanted much more for myself, but subconsciously I did not believe I could get there on my own. I stayed, using the excuse of wanting my sons raised in a two-parent home. Not wanting my sons to experience what I had been through when my parents got divorced. But I began to see it was more important to show my children what healthy love looked like, rather than the dysfunctional love I had grown up with.

It was important for me to show my sons that their mother would not compromise her values for a wealthy lifestyle. That became my WHY, and still holds true today.

I saw a glimmer of hope for our future. My story would not end in a constant cycle of two steps towards happy, five steps back into the narcissistic hell that I had lived in for so many years.

I realized that I had prescribed to all the social bullshit of, "Honey, sometimes you have to put up with a little something when you're dealing with (insert some wealthy profession/wealthy man).", or "All men act like that, but he still loves you." or "All relationships are hard." or the best yet, "It's better to have a piece of a man than nothing at all."

I called bullshit on all of it and on all the generational lies! I set out to prove that I experienced those narcissistic relationships for a reason even though I had no idea what it was. I decided that if I had to go through the fire, it would make me stronger and more beautiful. I decided to declare I was receiving beauty for the
ashes of the person I had been, and I would claim my inheritance of prosperity!

So many of the ladies I work with now experience PTSD after narcissistic abuse. I wanted to delve more into post-traumatic growth. What could the process of rebuilding and leveling up after narcissistic abuse really look like? How could I go from victim to victorious? I want people to know, I don't need a hug, I need a way to rebuild!

Don't get me wrong. There were plenty of times when I felt my subconscious was fighting me every step of the way. I had such low self-worth that I literally laughed at my dreams when they popped into my head. I had forgotten how to dream, and that triggered me because I felt so ashamed for settling. I knew that in order for me to powerfully co-create and manifest with God again, I had to figure out a way to learn how to dream and allow myself to dream big again.

I know now that the journey of rebuilding after narcissism never ends like a recovered addict remains an addict for the rest of their life. Knowing this, I became engrossed in documenting the things, large and small, that helped me regain my confidence and allowed prosperity back into my life. The things that re-connected me to my purpose because standard inner work does not work for someone that has experienced narcissistic abuse.

All of the self-help gurus were telling me to look in the mirror and say, "I love myself". But how do you do that when the one you love the most makes you feel unworthy of love?

It takes a special type of care to rebuild after this type of abuse. I was fascinated with the number of high-powered, ambitious, loving, successful, and outwardly strong women I knew who had been robbed of their inner worth by a narcissist and did not even realize it because they too had been conditioned to believe that this was love and they just had a "difficult" partner.

To the beautiful goddess reading this, know that your experience of a toxic relationship in your past is not wasted. Know that you have it in you to rebuild yourself and create a life that you are in love with. If I were stepping back into that younger version of myself trapped in a relationship with a narcissist and looking to escape or have left that kind of abusive relationship but are wondering "Now what?". Pay attention! I am going to tell you what I would do if I were you.

First, figure out a way to make your own money!

90% of women coming out of narcissism leave with no money, usually because they do not feel worthy of anything anymore. You need to feel worthy to be able to retain your confidence, wealth, happiness, all those positive things that will help you rebuild and then to maintain. Having access to your own money will give you the confidence to rebuild your life after leaving a narcissist, and to begin to live your life on your terms.

Secondly, realize that those narcissistic abusive relationships happened FOR us, not TO us and there is a very important lesson in everything you have gone through, every experience. You are so much stronger for surviving that relationship! See your survival as the triumph it is, and you will continue to triumph!

It is crucial that you sit in a safe space and visualize yourself living a life you love. See yourself being successful in all areas of your life, on your own terms. Because if we have to rebuild, DAMMIT we are rebuilding on our own terms! We are rebuilding massively! No more playing small in any area of our life! Believe in the promises that God, Universe, Source, whatever human name you put on the great I AM, has made, and have asked you to hold him accountable for.
Forging this connection to this vision of your future self is very important in rebuilding because there are going to be times when you are going to be overwhelmed. When you are going to be confused about your future.

You have to find a way to shift the perception of that energy from fear and figuring out the "how" to trust in God and become filled with excitement for the possibilities of what is to come.

Ultimately, connecting to this vision for yourself will lead you to re-discovering your purpose, which is the key to living life on your terms and standing firm in that vision with confidence.

Reframe your perception of yourself. Move from victim to victorious and focus on an attitude of empowerment. Learn to live the brave way!

Tierra Womack – Confidence & Wealth Coach

How unbecoming of me.

Standing with our arms wrapped around each other. Trembling, my stomach in knots, my eyes closed, tears streaming down my face. I opened my eyes. It was still there. That huge, obnoxious piece of art he had promised to remove. After endless arguments about getting rid of "Her" stuff. She was everywhere. "It's going to be okay." He repeated in my ear. But it was not. I had to leave. Still hoping he would beg me to stay, keep his promises and "choose" me.

I left that day, my heart broken. With no plan other than to pack up and drive 22 hours back home to Utah.

I had had many failed relationships, but this was different. So much love and passion, but also such pain. When things were good, they were amazing; but I never knew who would show up. The man who loved and adored me, or the accuser who might leave and shut down, refusing my calls.

I accommodated his insecurities and extreme jealousy. Took care of the needs and care of his three children. Put up with his ex-wife, coming and going as she pleased, still orchestrating his life. "Go along with this, and I will give you the world," he said. The world? I just wanted kindness. For four years I put up with incessant arguments, sleepless nights, and many tears. Followed by empty apologies and unkept promises.

I lost myself in those four years. I did not recognize myself. Who had I become?

Walking away was the hardest thing I have ever done. This was the beginning of my un-becoming. I fell apart.

Alone for the first time in my life. Terrified. My heart heavy. Replaying "happy" memories over and over. Looking through photographs, re-reading emails and texts. Missing him terribly, wishing he would "wake up". Realize what he had lost. Anger and confusion set in. "How could I let this happen to me?" It took everything in me not to reach out, and sometimes I failed. I reached out to other men, desperate to be wanted, searching for validation. Lost in the story of "why me."

One sleepless, drunken, tearful night, I dropped to my knees and asked God to help me. I had not prayed in years. I pleaded with Him to take away the pain, to make it all go away. I wanted to be the happy, carefree girl I once was. I suppose this was my "dark night of the soul." The night I realized I would never be the same.

Truthfully, I did not want to be *that* girl. Allowing herself to be treated badly. Lurching from one failed relationship to another. That night, I listened to my heart and knew that things had to change.

Who was I? And how did I get here?

I grew up in a house with six kids, filled with love and laughter. My parents were affectionate and loving. Dad and mom, dancing in the kitchen, kissing and twirling. There was a lot of passion between them, good and bad. I was nine when my mom had an affair and left.

Unfortunately, my dad thought I should be privy to all the unpleasant details. My mom was my world. I was hurt and confused. They divorced. It was ugly. My dad remarried within a year, divorced her, and then remarried my mom. All within three years. Inevitably, after years of fighting, my parents divorced again when I was 14. Many attempts to reconcile followed.

I learned to take care of myself because mom and dad were caught up in their own drama. It was a lonely time. Being a typical 16-year-old girl, my boyfriend became everything to me. I got pregnant on my 17th birthday. Raised in the Mormon faith, I did "the proper thing" and we got married.

Having said that I would never end up like my mother, there I was, walking the same path.

Eighteen-years-old with a little one, and a husband who came home every day exhausted from a job he hated. I was a working mom, also trying to be a good dutiful wife. I was miserable. I left when my son was only 11 months old, and I broke his dad's heart.

I jumped straight into another relationship, and another after that, leaving them both broken hearted.

Then He came along; challenging me in ways I had not been challenged before. I felt new things. I said, "You're going to fall in love with me." He did and the feelings were mutual. Religious and cultural differences caused him to end it. He realized he had made a mistake and begged me try again, offering to convert, do whatever it took. I never let him close again.

History repeated itself; eleven months in I was pregnant. My fiancé was big in stature, intelligent, quiet, and reserved. He made me feel safe, a father figure. I convinced myself that this was "meant to be." I packed up my life, left my family and everything I knew, and moved to Chicago to start a new life.

Again, trying to make things work, trying to be happy, to be a good wife and mother. I was so happy when I gave birth to my daughter. I love being a mother. The happiness did not last long. I was 26, working a job I hated to make ends meet, and taking care of a household by myself. My husband struggled with depression. I did not understand or have patience for it. Things unraveled quickly. I left, 4 years into the marriage, and found myself in the arms of another man.

He was completely the opposite of my ex. We had a nice life, very social. We were the best of friends but sadly, not the best of lovers. I felt safe again, in a different way. With him I did not feel exposed and vulnerable. Desperate to create a family for my children I married him. Thinking, "I will make this work." That marriage lasted 5 years. Like my parents, we tried to reconcile for many years following our divorce.

There were other relationships, but they all ended with me feeling unhappy and unsettled.

I gave up on love, creating a narrative that "I was too much" and "no man could make me happy."

Then I met him—my soulmate.

The connection was immediate. Drawn to him in an inexplicable way, I felt things in my body I had not experienced before. I was all in, heart and soul. This was my greatest lesson - my Unbecoming. I did not understand at the time because I had been lost in heartache and confusion for so long.

Now, I understand. I needed him to wake me up, to let light into the darkness inside. To begin to heal the wounds of a little girl who believed love was unreliable and fleeting and that people would always leave eventually.

We all have a soulmate(s). Some come into our lives for a short time, others stay a lifetime. It is important we understand every relationship is 'meant for us', but that doesn't mean it is meant to last.

He was meant for me. He is my soulmate. I am grateful for him and send him love every day.

The road to healing was not easy. The common denominator in all my failed relationships, was me. Operating with a broken belief system I needed to start showing myself the deep, loving compassion I needed.

"Maybe the journey isn't so much about becoming anything, maybe it's about unbecoming everything that isn't really you so you can be who you were really meant to be in the first place." – Paul Coelho

Through my unbecoming, I abandoned the story I had been telling myself "I have relationship issues." Stopped looking outside myself for validation. No longer allowed a relationship or a man to define me and my life. I began to trust myself. Began to believe I *would* find a loving partner to share my life with.

Today, I am madly and deeply in love with the kindest, smartest, funniest man. We are best friends and share deep intimacy. I feel cherished and blessed.

When we met, I was honest about my past. Three failed marriages doesn't make for the greatest first impression! But I had let go of my story and any shame I held about my past. Having worked to heal my beliefs about love and relationships, I was able to show up fully in my truth. He struggled with trust because of his past, so he found it refreshing that I could share so openly.

I became very clear about what I wanted. It was not about being a mom, creating a family or fixing things to make them work. I wanted a man committed to his own growth and evolving in a conscious partnership.

We discovered our core values were fundamentally aligned. I envisioned the life I wanted to create and shared it with him, and it became clear our vision for the future was the same.

I found the love I always desired. It was no longer from the "need" of that little, wounded girl - it was from this deep knowing that I am inherently worthy, whole, and complete.

Sweetheart. Know that you are worthy, whole, and complete. Nothing outside of you - not a man or relationship – can give that to you or take it away. The relationship you have with yourself is the most important one. It will reflect in all other relationships. When you learn to love and accept yourself in all of your messy and magnificent humanness, you will find a partner who will reflect that love back to you.

Remember, *you* are the common denominator in your relationships. Look at your life with loving curiosity, not judgment.

Here are some journal prompts to help you gain clarity:

- What examples did my caregivers model in love and relationship? Was there communication? Were feelings allowed and expressed or swept under the rug? Was there fighting, degradation, disrespect? What have I normalized through my learning and conditioning?
- What did love look and feel like. How is that reflected in my relationship(s)?
- As a child, was love present, kind, nurturing or was it uncertain? Were my emotions ignored? Was life safe or chaotic? What feels familiar to what I learned in my relationship(s)?
- Who did I have to be in order to receive love and praise? The "good girl", quiet and dismissive, the "people pleaser?" I am a recovering people pleaser.

This is not about blaming your parents; it is about waking up to how you have been unconsciously showing up in your relationships. Taking ownership, taking your power back. Through this awareness, you get to choose which qualities of mom/dad/caregivers are your truth, and which are not—the Unbecoming.

If our fundamental needs were not met as a child, as an adult it is our responsibility to hold that little girl with love and compassion and tell her what she needs to hear. You learn to show up for yourself and begin to trust yourself creating love and safety from within.

Imagine yourself as that little girl. See her and be with her. Place your hands on your heart and visualize those moments when she felt dismissed, when she was frightened and alone, felt she was not enough. What did she need to hear?

Example: Sweetheart, it is okay, you are safe. You are loved. I am here for you; you are not alone. You are worthy of love, kindness, and respect. You are powerful and beautiful, inside, and out.

Showing up for yourself in this way is empowering. Your beliefs about not being worthy will shift.

Do you know your core values? What do you value in yourself and in life? Your core values are your compass, guiding you through life. In relationships, it is important for you both to be fundamentally aligned with your values. If your values are different, it can create a disconnected, unhealthy dynamic.

Whenever I am in doubt, I repeat my core values, remind myself of my truth to gain clarity on how to move forward.

What do you truly desire? Your heart's desires are the roadmap for what is meant for you - do not dismiss them. Many women are afraid to declare what they want because they do not feel worthy. Allow yourself to envision what you want, even if it feels uncomfortable at first. Close your eyes, create a mental picture in your mind. What does it look like, and more importantly, how does it feel? Write it down, in detail.

The mind does not know the difference between fantasy and reality. Our thoughts and beliefs create our existence. This exercise, practiced consistently, will help you be clear about how you want to feel in a relationship. Change the lens through which you experience yourself and the world. You will believe love is meant for you and manifest the love you desire.

Sweetheart, you are not broken. Nothing needs fixing. No-one and nothing outside of you will complete you. You are whole and perfect, right now. All the answers you seek are within you. Stop searching outside of yourself and begin to hold up that loving mirror. Instead of tearing yourself down, get curious; get to know your true self. Go beyond your conditioning, learned behaviors and trauma. Meet those parts of you that you hide in shame, with radical self-acceptance. Learn to love that little girl inside you. Show up powerfully for her (you). Stop modifying who you are or trying to make something 'fit.' Get clear about the love and life you want to create. No more waiting to be "chosen"—choose YOU. Make the relationship with yourself the ultimate, most cherished relationship you have. Life will mirror all that love back to you. Knowing how inherently worthy you are, embodied in your essence and truth, you will attract a partner who will honor and appreciate all that you are.

Here's to love, the one thing we all seek from the beginning to the end of our days. And here's to the greatest love - the most prolific love story of all - the love and relationship you have with yourself.

Karli Kershaw – Relationship & Inner Work Coach

Be ok being open, raw, and vulnerable.

The unravelling of me, and everything I thought I was. Everything I had believed in. And finding my way home... To me!

Have you ever woken up and thought to yourself what has today got in store for me? Or here we go again? Or said to yourself, I cannot take any more pain or drama today?

I did. And still do, some days...

I have doubted who I was, and who I am. I have had days full of self-hatred and loathing, self-pity, and self-doubt. Feeling lost and lonely, afraid of my own shadow. Afraid of becoming the woman I truly wanted to be.

I built my walls high and kept myself small. I could not speak out loud or voice my opinions because I thought I had nothing to say that would matter to those around me.

I was never the kind of girl who planned out my life in the tiniest of detail. But I did keep notebooks full of my heart's hopes, dreams, and ideas that I hoped would one day come true.

My early life was shrouded with hurt and shame.

Shame of being the girl who lived with a mother that was beaten every day. By the man who was my dad.

Shame when your dreams are torn from your heart when your dad leaves your 5-year-old self without a goodbye or a backwards glance.

Shame for being the young girl who was sexually abused, and again when that led to being bullied and beaten all through my younger years.

Shame for being the girl who was told, you are useless, you are ugly, you should never have been born.

Shame for the self-hatred, self-doubt, and the eating disorder that started because I just wanted the hurt to stop.

And hurt because that little girl, aged 5, felt powerless to stop it all from happening. The burden of looking after myself, my little brother, and my mum was too big some days for my little shoulders.

But I did it. I became the carer, the nurturer, the people pleaser. With a smile and a laugh that hid the tears, the trauma, and the heartache. I did it because I did not know I had a choice.

So, I grew up always feeling the odd one out, the one left on the side-lines. I would compare myself to the other kids, who had both a mum and a dad that loved and protected them from the hurts and pain of life.

I did my best to fit in. I was the girl who always went the extra mile. Doing as I was told because I wanted to be liked and loved. I wanted to live in a world where people did not hate me. Because I already hated myself.

I went on to more controlling, abusive, and hurtful relationships that left me a shadow of the girl I longed to be.

It was exhausting and left me feeling shite about myself 24/7.

So how do you heal from the heartbreak and the pain? How do you soothe that hurt child that resides in your soul How do you rescue yourself, while life goes on around you? When you desperately need to rest. When all you want is to sit without thinking or feeling anything at all.

But you can't. Because you are a wife, a sister, a daughter, a friend, a mum. Who has four children of her own. You put your life on hold. Because they need you, as they have special needs and disabilities, and there is no help or support with the tiredness and the meltdowns.

There is chaos and endless juggling of all the roles you must play. Teacher, taxi driver, counsellor, playmate, soulmate, and lover. There are a million and one different things that all this involves that can bring you to your knees. What do you do?

You long for just 5 minutes of peace. But you plaster on a smile and you say it's ok, I am fine.

Feeling sad, scared, ashamed, guilty, and angry. But the sheer shitty loneliness is by far the hardest thing to deal with. It takes you by the throat and hangs you out to dry.

A life lived in the shadow of violence, loss and heartache leaves you shattered by the force of the emotions that hit you time, and time again throughout your life.

But what do you do? You carry on of course. Because you think you should!

But for me, everything changed, the year I lost you. A fragment of my soul, my heart shredded into tiny pieces. Tears running down my cheeks because I had to let you go. You changed not just my world, but your sisters too.

A decision made without knowing if it was the right one. A decision made with nothing but love for you. To lose you hurt me. Little did I know just a month after I would lose my north, the one woman. Who had always had my back since birth.

Nan you died suddenly in your sleep. I never got the chance to tell you I love you, say thank you, or goodbye. But you did get to help me from beyond the grave, one last time.

Alone in the house, looking at my computer screen. Looking at the coaching courses I had coveted for so long. Wishing and dreaming; What if? You whispered words in my ear, and literally pushed me off my chair. Your time is now, you have come so far It is time to take a stand and show them who you are.

Nan, thank you for your guiding hand, from my cradle to your grave. You gave me the courage to try and be me...

And then in 2020 the Covid-19 pandemic broke

Curveballs continued coming, with parents who decided to keep overstepping my boundaries. Telling lies that could destroy lives, and not just mine. I took a stand to speak my truth and lost my brother in the fight.

After everything else, it was too much, and I lost the will to fight. I could not carry on being everyone else's protector. My inner light faded, and I lost the desire to do anything other than go through the motions.

But my soul continued to seek something more.

My inner flame refused to go out and I continued to dream of a better life, of making a change. But everyone tells you, do not make decisions when you are grieving.

Still a part of me kept encouraging me to keep my dreams alive. Reminding me that yes, my past may have shaped me, but it does not define who I am.

I used meditation and reiki to release and let go, to be free from the judgement that was destroying me. The sessions made me laugh so hard at times, I cried. Sharing a part of my past, that I had never told anyone about before. Seeing her face in that moment, shocked because laughing was not perhaps the most appropriate way of reacting. But for me it was the release of a burden I was not aware I still carried.

I had always felt alone, had never felt as though I had the help and support that I needed. These sessions opened a door, and it all came tumbling out. In one hot mess.

I will always be grateful for her and those sessions because she allowed me too just be... ME!

It is possible to keep all the painful memories and all the challenges you have faced locked inside a box. Contained and out of sight. I know because I did.

And for the millionth time in a bloody row, you will ask yourself: Is this it? Is this all my life was ever meant to be? Surrounded by shadows of the past?

In the past few years, I have turned to personal development. First as a dancer where I got to competition level. Then writing as a co-author in my first book. And now this, my 2nd book.

Now I use spirituality, writing, and personal development as a way to help me heal. To elevate my own soul growth.

I have qualified as a life, spiritual and happiness coach, journal therapist, and an angelic guide. I am an energy healer and teacher. I use my different modalities to guide overwhelmed mums and heart-centred females to reclaim their self-identity and rewrite their stories.

And though I may look back on my past life with some tears, regret and heartache I will not say I am sorry because it has led me to the here and now. To today. A good place to be.

I am not an expert on trauma, drama, or dealing with curveballs But I have lived my life filled with shadows and fear. Fear so bad that some days it has really brought me to my knees. Found me begging, no more, not today, I cannot take the pain.

However, I refuse to be sad, for my life has also given me strength, laughter, and resilience. And has given me the courage to say, I now know my soul purpose.

And your story, your life's journey will not be the same as mine, or anyone else's for that matter, we are all different. All unique and beautiful in our own way.

My hope for my journey and chapter within this book Is that it may resonate with your heart and inspire you to know that is for everyday goddesses everywhere.

To know that life is not perfect.

To know that it is ok to feel, think and act, how you need to, in any given moment. There is no right or wrong way.

There is no normal, or perfect.

What does that even mean anyway? For me it does not exist.

But being beautifully vulnerable, open, raw, kind, and soul-hearted does.

Because although our past may shape us, it does not define us. Our history is not who we are. It is not about being a victim, or a story of grief. I have learned the hard way, that life will always throw us curveballs.

The trick is to bend without breaking.

It is about peeling back the layers, to see what's underneath.

To know your thoughts are fleeting and that you have a choice.

It is about taking time to uncover what matters to you and your soul truth.

Soul Powered Journal Prompts

Start by asking yourself:

- How do I want to feel each and every day?
- What makes me feel happy and soul fulfilled?
- When and where am I at my happiest?
- If failure was not an option, what would I do with my life?
- What changes do I need to make, to live my dream life?
- Where do I want to be, and what do I want to be doing 5 years from now?

Listen to your heart and the whispers within.

Gift yourself the space and time to process all that your life has already been.

Get ready to stand in your soul power, it is time to begin.

Lisa Martin – Curveball Queen

Consciously nourishing your mind, body, and soul.

"You're so stupid."

"No wonder everyone hates you."

"You're so weak and overly sensitive. Nobody will ever love you."

"You're fat. If you could just lose some weight..."

Hurtful words, but these are not coming from bullies. They are inside my own head. They are loud and they never stop.

Pop another painkiller for the headache, avoid another meal, drink another drink at the weekend. Numb the body, control the weight, and drown out the mind.

As a twenty-something my happiness lies in the hands of everything outside of me - what people think of me; what I weigh; how little I can eat; and what I can achieve to make *other* people proud of me and respect me, to be worth something.

But looking at the numbers on the scale dipping below yet another goal, I do not feel happy or have any sense of achievement. Maybe a little bit lighter, a little more likeable, I will try a little bit harder...

Fast forward ten years and things are not too dissimilar.

I have a gorgeous daughter now; I always wanted to be a Mama and love it and her to bits but there is still something missing. I have a career and work at a great company with lovely people but still do not feel any sense of achievement or fulfilment. I am still searching for answers and things to lift me and fix me.

I am struggling to have another baby; it is just not happening for me and I am so angry at my body for letting me down. I have so much to be grateful for but still feel so lost, I feel so guilty about that.

I want the doctors to give me answers, to tell me what to do so my family can be complete, to make me complete.

- If I can just get pregnant *then* I will feel happy.
- Why is my body doing this *to* me?
- Do I not deserve another baby?

- I feel powerless, life is happening to me and around me.

If you flash forward another 10 years things **are** very different but let's not get to that yet. I want to start with a question...

Are you outsourcing your health and happiness?

It took that moment of complete powerlessness to realise that I had spent decades doing exactly that.

Our health. As a teen I was put on the contraceptive pill to minimise monthly pain, then on beta blockers for anxiety, then antidepressants for, you guessed it, depression. When I started to have issues with back pain - super strong painkillers and anti-inflammatories. Then more pills to counteract the negative effects of those. Nobody ever talked to me about alternatives. Just sweep the symptoms under the carpet and carry on. It seemed to be the normal way. I do not blame the doctors; they are doing the job they are trained to do. It is this culture we have of compartmentalising aspects of ourselves and viewing our bodies as just this thing to fix, rather than part of our whole.

Our happiness. Where does it come from? If you are like I was, then maybe your happiness comes from making others happy, from feeling valued or appreciated by others. I craved external validation and wanted everyone to like me, everyone to value me because it was the only way I valued myself. I did not trust my own judgement.

My sense of worth hinged on how I anticipated others felt about me and were speaking about me, yet I was speaking to myself worse than any school bully I ever encountered.

Everywhere we look we are told what to do to be healthy, or slim, or attractive, or happy. Take this tablet, follow this diet, do this fitness regime, use this make up, practice gratitude daily. The latest trend or the latest drug, it is all the same - we give away our power to blindly follow, ever hopeful that this will be the one thing that "fixes" us but if we are not emotionally engaged or doing what is right for US, it just ends up being another fail on our list.

It took me two decades of outsourcing my own health, both mental and physical, before I decided enough was enough and took back control.

Seeds of holistic health had already been planted the moment I knew I was pregnant with my first child.

Being pregnant forces you to look at your choices - are you getting the nourishment the baby needs? On one hand it was terrifying, as I suddenly felt invisible, like just an incubator for the baby, but on the other hand a deep sense of responsibility to look after myself for my unborn daughter.

I was adamant that no daughter of mine would ever grow up hating her body. Yet after she was born, I found myself slipping back into my old habits. Obsessing over my baby weight, restricting my food, and talking badly to myself. Between the post-baby hormone chaos, not enough sleep and not finding time to take care of myself, whilst juggling work and Mum guilt it is safe to say I spiralled. When we had trouble falling pregnant the second time, I had to take a real look at my health. Was I really looking after myself? I ate well and exercised but why? Truth be told it was all about weight, not really about my health.

Was I really caring for my mind? Nope, failing there too. Telling myself daily that I was a failure; a bad mum for working, not good enough at my job because I was a mum, that my body was letting me down.

In my thirties I finally learned about our monthly cycle and hormones, I learned to truly nourish my body, give it what it needed. I embraced yoga and meditation, I made time to do the things that made me feel strong and healthy and allowed myself time to rest. I have my daughter to thank for that, if it were not for her, I may well have never started this journey.

What I discovered was that health and happiness are pretty simple - do what makes us FEEL good, what we are guided to and it all just falls into place.

Now, in my 40's I have a completely different approach to my wellness. Not because I follow any particular rules, but because I learned to follow my heart. It took time to tune back into my body, to become one with it rather than at war. To reconnect to my soul and hear what it was telling me.

I eat mainly plant based but do not label or restrict, I eat what I want to eat and what my body needs. I have an apothecary of powders and herbs because they make me feel my best, not because of any promises they make.

I do not "exercise" anymore, I move in ways that make me feel good. I go for a walk to clear my head, practice yoga, swim, or paddle board. I love being by water, it equals instant calm for me.

I know the signs my mental health is on the decline; I can spot when low moods are hanging around and I have a myriad of holistic tools I can draw on.

There are no rules in my life these days, no labels but **a lot** of self-awareness. Checking in to see what I need at any given time.

I know what every woman should know - that you ALWAYS know best what is right FOR YOU. You might need some help tuning in and discovering what that is, but I believe the key to health and happiness is finding the things that light you up and make you feel good.

Here is the truth: Self-awareness and self-care are key, both to your happiness and health. You can be your own guru; you already know what you need - you just need to listen.

For me personally, yoga was the starting point for the transformation of my relationship with my body, my mind, my soul, and my overall mental and physical health. What started as a practice tied to my body image issues, shifted over time to a practice that brought me comfort and love for my body, calm to my mind and re-connected me to my intuition. It was not until I completed my yoga teacher-training that I started to understand why yoga holds such magic. And how even the physical aspect works through the layers of our subtle energy body. It is this intrinsic link between our energy body and physical body that is fundamental to its transformational quality.

We have developed phrases such as "weight of the world on your shoulders" or "butterflies in the tummy" to describe certain emotional states showing up in your body. But where do these come from? There is an intrinsic link between what we feel in our bodies and what is going on energetically and emotionally for us. Something Louise Hay beautifully discussed in You Can Heal Your Life, in her list of ailments and related emotional causes.

When we do not listen to our emotions, when we ignore our niggles of intuition and push them away, so we can carry on, that is when they start to show up in our physical body. Maybe subtly to begin with, getting louder and louder until we take notice. At our core we are spiritual beings having a human experience, it makes sense to me now that any disease, any physical ailments are tied to something far deeper at a soul level.

If you are sick and tired of outsourcing your health and happiness, where should you start?

Do not let the ambition of where you want to be overwhelm you and stop you from starting. Start small and take the first steps and watch the universe support and encourage you to continue.

1 - Reconnect with yourself

Find ways to reconnect with yourself, free from expectations and judgements. For me, that is on my yoga mat either in a physical yoga practice or meditation.

Mindful movement with breath such as yoga or tai chi will work with your physical and energy body and land you back in your body, really connected. Yoga is often translated as "union" and this union of mind, body and soul is the key to better understanding ourselves and what it is we need.

2 - Re-define health

I am going to be blunt here: Your weight does not equal your health.

How can you move your body that feels good?

What would a healthy mind and soul look like to you?

If we reconsider our body as the home for our soul, a spark of the divine, then how should we treat her?

Try swapping some terms in the way you refer to these and see what difference it makes to your thoughts on health:

Restriction > Nurturing

Exercise > Movement

Weight > Health

Look > Feel

3 - Make friends with your intuition

Many of us lose touch with our intuition as we grow up. We push it aside for "logical and smart" decisions, often guided by well-meaning loved ones or general societal norms. Do not beat yourself up if you feel your inner compass has been lost for good, I promise it is still there, and you can reconnect with it. The more you use it the easier it gets.

Practices that support your heart chakra and your third eye will help you to connect into choosing from your heart and allowing guidance to flow.

Start small - if you are someone who usually weighs up the pros and cons before you can even make a decision on what coffee or lunch to order - stop. Read the menu. Close your eyes and pause to take a breath. What immediately springs to mind? Order that. No need to re-read over and over, your answer is already there – it has popped in so let it be. Enjoy it, savour it and thank your intuition for making such a good and delicious choice!

In my experience both personally, and from working with many women, is that your initial thought, reaction, or opinion rarely leads you astray. Be mindful of noticing these feelings. The more you follow them the more you will be greeted with opportunities and decisions that bring joy into your life.

Finally - TRUST Yourself.

Follow those nudges, move with joy, nurture don't deprive, and you will thrive. You will find a sense of purpose and with that meaning and happiness, you will have a body that more loved and loving in return. Your mind will be your friend, not your enemy. Trust yourself, the rest will follow.

Michelle Maslin-Taylor – Holistic Therapist and Yoga Teacher

The witch wound.

Women are waking up. They are realising that they are not designed for the modern, capitalist, competitive, consumerist world created by men hundreds of years ago. They are hungry for something more, something deeper.

The driving and striving, hurry and worry, pushing and rushing just is not working anymore. Women in particular are experiencing record levels of burnout and stress-related health issues. All as a result of trying to keep up with a way and pace of life that is not in alignment with who they truly are, and surviving on a cocktail of adrenalin, caffeine, and wine! (I have been there).

I have worked with tens of thousands of awakening women all over the world for over 20 years. The patterns and stories are all similar. I see intelligent, strong, gifted women struggling to feel fulfilled. Women passionate about living their purpose and potential, but not trusting themselves, or each other. They have tried everything, spent a fortune on courses and mentoring but something always holds them back. They keep burning out, sliding backwards and feel ashamed. Blaming themselves, they think they are just not good enough. Or they stay in hiding, in the spiritual closet, suppressing their gifts out of fear.

But why is this? Why are so many women struggling to thrive, and live the life they know they are meant for?

Well, firstly our biology, brain, and nervous system, of all genders and sexes, is still pretty much where it was millions of years ago. We are designed for a gentler, more natural way of life, close to Mother Earth and her cycles and seasons. It is only relatively recently that the industrial revolution began a period of rapid technological evolution and completely changed how we live. Advances are happening very quickly and yet our bodies, hearts, and souls long for, and are designed for, something much more natural and Divine.

Secondly, around 1600 years ago, Roman emperor Constantine planted some of the first seeds of patriarchy and began to erase Goddess culture and women from religion and history. This led to a world based on wounded masculine energy ways of living and working, more suited to men and their energy, biology, and psychology, than to women and their ways of being. It quickly became the dominant new normal.

Before that, our world lived in an earth and nature-based culture, centred around respect and reverence for women, for the ways of the Sacred Feminine and of the Goddess. Our world was very much based on equality, justice, respect for nature and the different local, indigenous traditions and spiritual lineages. We had 200,000 years as humans, rooted in nature, guided by the stars and moon cycles, growing food, supporting community, and working closely with our ancestral traditions, beliefs, and spirituality.

Then suddenly Goddess culture and Herstory was edited and erased and led to the persecution and execution of anyone who did not follow the newly branded monotheistic patriarchal Christian church. The Feminine was no longer welcome or safe. Girls and women were killed just for picking herbs or growing food with the cycles of the moon. They were prosecuted for gathering in a sacred circle, or just for knowing someone rumoured to be intuitive or a wise woman. Women were turned against each other to spare their lives, causing a deep sisterhood wound of mistrust, that still affects women's relationships today.

This period of history has been referred to as the 'Women's Holocaust'. A conservative estimate is that hundreds of thousands of women and girls were killed during the witch hunts that spanned hundreds of years during the Middle Ages.

The impact of the mass killing of women by men who feared their feminine, spiritual, intuitive and sexual power, created a traumatic imprint, a deep wound that women still carry today, and which has led to an internalised fear and suppression of intuitive gifts and of the Sacred Feminine inside and out. The buried rage women carry is affecting reproductive health. The background hum of trauma is keeping women disconnected from themselves and their bodies, their nervous systems are in a heightened state of survival mode (fight, flight, freeze or fawn) all of which blocks natural intuitive, creative, and sexual power. All the 'Build a six-figure soulful business in 3 months' courses in the world won't work if you don't address the Feminine Wound, ancestral wounds, tend to the trauma and come home to yourself first. We need strong roots to be able to grow far and wide without falling over.

Modern epigenetics reveals that such a trauma can be passed down through generations from our ancestors who were alive in those 'burning times'. When we have a past life flashback or regression, we may in fact be witnessing deep memory from our bloodline or experiencing information held in the collective field. So even if you have not had a major traumatic event in this lifetime, you could still be affected by an inherited and/or collective trauma.

Modern culture is based on old wounded masculine templates and it has caused soul loss in women, disconnection from our bodies and a mistrust of our own inner knowing and power. I have seen it in myself, in my own maternal line and in over 20,000 clients I have worked with over the last 20 years.

The Feminine Wound is passed down the maternal line. Research into trauma and DNA reveals that these inherited patterns can lead to health issues via the Mitochondria, the DNA from the mother. For me personally the inherited Feminine Wound manifested as Fibromyalgia (considered a Mitochondrial condition), Chronic Fatigue and complex trauma.

So, I wonder, is the huge rise of Fibromyalgia, Chronic Fatigue, M.E., Adrenal Exhaustion and burn-out a direct outcome of the Feminine Wound and the suppression of the Goddess in a patriarchally created modern world that does not support or honour the Feminine? Food for thought.

The Witch Wound
I am a highly sensitive, Clairvoyant, Clairsentient energy intuitive, empath and natural born Shaman. So I read and understand the deeper layers and patterns of energy and information of life. I see the Quantum Field and read the Akashic fields across space and time. For many years I had a private healing practice in an integrative and complimentary medicine clinic run by a British medical doctor. I conducted thousands of intuitive energy scans of mainly women. 95 percent of those scans revealed a particular energy pattern in the bodies of those women.

As I observed these energy patterns and activated healing energy in those areas, the women resting on my treatment couch would have strong experiences, emotions, flashbacks, and sensations in their bodies. These flashbacks were 'memories' of being killed for living and practising the natural ways of the

Goddess. They recalled being executed as a Witch and seeing others being hunted and killed. They saw clear memories or felt strong feelings of fear. In fact, my clients often came to me feeling so much fear about using their intuition or accessing their spiritual power that they thought they might die. They knew it did not make sense but did not know where the feelings were coming from.

Discovering it was deep memory, ancestral trauma and part of the Feminine Wound gave them such a sense of validation and gave them somewhere to start exploring and healing so they could finally access their full potential and lost Sacred Feminine power.

This deep ancestral, collective trauma related to our feminine power and in particular our intuitive gifts is what I named The Witch Wound. Of the 95 percent of my clients who held patterns of the Witch Wound in their energy system, 100 percent of those presented this wound around their throat. Why? Because we were silenced, our voices were suppressed, when we spoke out it cost lives. No wonder so many of us struggle now to step up and speak out and share our gifts and our truth. I hear clients regularly say they are afraid of their power; afraid they will do more harm than good if they come out of the spiritual closet and start sharing their truth and awakening their gifts.

I come from a long line of Clairvoyant Mediums. I grew up watching my Mother read Tarot and tea leaves and observing my Great-Grandmother mentor her. But it was all behind closed doors and shrouded in fear. My Father, who came from a religious Christian family, would get enraged when she used her gifts, the outcome was always violent and bloody. When my gifts opened fully at around the age of 4 and I started seeing and communicating with spirits, all hell broke loose in our home and I was rushed down to the church by my Father for a hurried christening and confirmation. There it was right there in my own home, persecution by the fearful masculine of the gifted feminine. The Witch Wound in action. But you know what? My Mother did her work anyway, as much as she could. It was an act of courage in the face of fear and violence. Despite her moments of courage, she passed the Witch Wound onto me, telling me not to follow this path. I dutifully suppressed my intuitive gifts, buried the Sacred Feminine, left my body and settled into my head and intellect.

I intuited the term 'Witch Wound' as a teenager and spent many years trying to find more information. It was not until I apprenticed with spiritual teachers, energy masters and a Shaman over 20 years ago that I came to understand the true nature of the Witch Wound and how this inherited collective trauma was holding women back and even making them unwell. The information was not readily available, the truth was suppressed, I hunted in library databases for years as a child and then searched on the early internet and found no reference to it.

So, I had to trust, to birth the wisdom myself. I did not realise at the time this was part of my own inner Goddess initiation, to follow my inner knowing and guidance and to trust that I was here to birth something new and important into the world in service of others, something that would spread like wildfire globally once I wrote my first blog about it many years ago.

My life's work is understanding and transforming the Feminine Wound and ancestral, collective trauma that blocks our embodiment of the Goddess and realisation of our true nature and to help women awaken and blaze in their own way. When we heal and transform the trauma of the Witch Wound and women rise once again, the world will change.

Messages and medicine from the Goddess
You were not born to strive, drive and just survive. You were made to flow, grow, and glow. You carry the legacy of both the wise and the wounded. You are the many faces of She. You are enough right now; you hold all the answers and contain the power. Your maternal line is rich with shadow codes and fertile templates of the new earth. Both are valid. To fully awaken, remember, reclaim, and transform, you do not need to go to some other realm or dimension or dissolve into oneness. The invitation is to ascend right here on Earth, grounding the light of the Divine in your daily life. Your mission is to both embody the light and face the shadows, to heal the ancestral wounds of your mothers and sisters before you, and come home to yourself, your body, your truth, your power, your gifts, your heart. I am you and you are me. You are the Goddess made flesh.

You carry the eternal memory, the blueprint of heaven on earth. You hold the seed of the radiant golden world we know deep down is possible. You carry the light in your blood. Patriarchy is falling. She is rising. This is your time. It is why you were born. You are enough. You are ready.

Kimberley Jones – Sacred Feminine Activist

Let Universal love flow generously into your life.

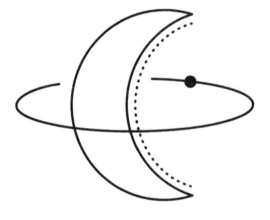

"As I began to love myself, I freed myself of anything that is no good for my health – food, people, things, situations, and everything that drew me down and away from myself. At first, I called this attitude a healthy egoism. Today I know it is "LOVE OF ONESELF".

-   *Charlie Chaplin*

Love has always been the strongest, most powerful force and gift in my life.

It is easy for me to love and give love to my children, partner, friends, family, my animals, or nature. It feels very natural and makes me happy to the core.

Growing up I realized that loving other people unconditionally is important. But loving ourselves in the same way is not something that we learned and can talk about openly. At least not in my family, and I hear the same from a lot of clients.

But why is it like that? Is it maybe too obvious? Of course we love ourselves; we do not need to focus on it, and stress the importance of it? Naturally, we strive for a supposedly perfect life, one in which we achieve our goals and realise our dreams. This can also be selfish at times. If everything in our life is going well, won't we love ourselves automatically? Not necessarily. The reason why it is hard to discuss "self-love" may be that it has a kind of an egoistic undertone and sounds a little inappropriate to people.

On my part it took a few profound events for me to get a deeper understanding about the concept of self-love. Before discovering the stability of self-love, I was fighting, making decisions out of fear, with deep regret for wrong choices I made and blaming myself all the time. Today I believe that self-love is the most important thing for any personal growth.

I was in the midst of ending an unhappy marriage and facing a very ugly drawn-out divorce. As a full-time working Mom, I was fighting to get shared custody of my children. But due to the law and my former husband's spiteful and revengeful behaviour, I did not stand a chance at that point.

I was heartbroken, my health was poor, my father had died, and I was in another unhealthy relationship. All this drove me into a deep mental and emotional crisis.

I remember one night clearly. I had just broken up with my boyfriend, missed my children terribly and my whole body was aching. My unbearable loneliness led to me laying sobbing on the bathroom floor. While I was laying there, I had the scary thought that ending my life was the only solution to stop the pain I was feeling.

I was wrong. And miraculously those thoughts I had, on that darkest night of my soul, marked the beginning of a new chapter in my life. I understood, that if there is a no one to blame, no one to share love with, and yet love still remained the most important thing in my life, I needed to "love the one you are with". That was me. And I started a new and vitally important relationship I ever had. With myself.

"To forgive is to set a prisoner free and discover that the prisoner was you"
   -   *Lewis Smedes*

Loving ourselves may actually be harder than loving someone else. Because we are the only person that knows ourselves inside out. It can be tough to love ourselves when we know everything about us, including all the unpleasant things.

I had a few sessions with Sara. She told me that she had problems loving herself fully concerning love relationships. She related this to a relationship she had had some years ago. She would still get hot and cold when she thought about how she was able to be with a man for such a long time. He cheated on her regularly. Even though she suspected it at the time, she stayed with him. She did not trust the intuition that was telling her right from the beginning of the relationship: Run!

Many years later, this was still affecting her. She still blamed him for doing this to her and blamed herself for staying with him. In our intense conversations, she quickly began to understand that she had a choice; whether to continue to suffer the after-effects of those experiences, or not.

In this process she saw for the first time that forgiveness is a cleansing agent that would allow her to move on with her life in a whole new way. Forgiveness does not mean that you approve of the negative behaviour from the other person. Rather, it means that you are no longer willing to carry around the toxic burden of anger inside you. And it was good for her to make this life-changing decision for herself! After all, it was she who suffered more from her anger and pain than anybody else.

It was important to forgive the part of her that said yes to the pain. Even if it was unconscious behaviour and something that she sustained longer than necessary.

Forgiving oneself requires you to change your thinking. And of course, back then Sara asked me: "Why should I forgive myself when I was the one who was hurt?"

I truly believe that only this way can one leave the existing pain and problems behind, and positively align the inner part of you that has been burdened with stress until now. At the end, there is an opportunity to love oneself and all parts of oneself. Even those that were previously connected with pain or rejection.

To summarise, people can do harmful things to us, but we can also harm ourselves. In return we respond in bad ways towards ourselves believing that we deserve it. And we blame ourselves too. Forgiving does not mean forgetting what happened. It means that the effect of someone else's behaviour, or our own, is not affecting us anymore. By letting go, and taking full responsibility for our part, we can free ourselves and open a door to a self-love that not only accepts the light and shines, but also the parts that we do not like, but ultimately also belong to us.

Take your time to figure out where you stand with loving yourself. Do not rush the inner work and dive deep: where do you need to let go, where do you need to take responsibility in your life, to make the shift towards the self-love you deeply hope for. Repeat and enjoy until it gets lighter. Take help from others, if necessary.

"I grow beyond my family's limitations and live for myself. It is my turn now."
- *Louise Hay*

Why are we so fixated on others and their opinions, when we ourselves are the person we spend most time within our lives? We should focus on loving and respecting ourselves first before we try to impress others. Of course, this is easier said than done. The need to be loved, rather than loving ourselves, can lead us to wrong decisions that can haunt us for a lifetime, if we do not change them and learn to trust our intuition again.

Judith was a banker. She came to see me, because her boss was not satisfied with her performance in her job and she hated herself for that reason and felt quite incompetent. She was sure that, if she were only good enough in her job, she would feel great and be able to love herself again. In a very natural way, she told me that all of her family worked in a bank or in the finance sector. It seemed to be a family tradition she followed. She was convinced that this was also her destiny. To me she came across as a very open, creative, lively, and playful person.

This observation brought me straight to the question: if her lack of self-love and esteem could be also a result of the wrong career choice and its effects. She burst into tears and told me what she had buried since childhood: her dream to become a kindergarten teacher. Her loyalty to her family made her choose a career in a bank. She told me that no one even expected her to do so.

Deep inside she ignored her true needs and denied the her? intuition that clearly told her from very early on to work with children. For many years she had suppressed these feelings. She did not want to disappoint anyone. Now she was at a point where she hated herself for having chosen this path. At this point, she was confronted with the wrong choice of career. The disastrous consequences of this decision took her far away from authenticity and self-love.

To go beyond the limitations, loyalty, and beliefs that our family has given to us is a very brave thing. At the same time, it is the most fundamental choice for feeding and nurturing our self-love. Judith did change her career. It was not easy, and it took some time, but when she finally did it and stood up for herself and her dreams, she was surprised what people that cared about her had to say.

They were full of joy and admiration for her decision and courage. Her self-love came back, a side effect on the choices she made for herself and her wellbeing.

If you feel stuck or unhappy in a job or a relationship go behind the scenes. Take your time to figure out if you or your family beliefs and limitations make you stay in a poor situation, instead of trusting your intuition by following your inner compass. Ask yourself is this situation just a challenge that will lead to growth or am I limiting myself and ignoring my intuition as a wise teacher?

Do not rush the inner work and dive deep: where do you need to trust your gut? Where do you need to take responsibility in your life to make the shift towards the self-love you deserve? Repeat and enjoy until you have more clarity. Take help from others, if necessary.

"There is always a light. If only we're brave enough to see it. If only we're brave enough to be it" - *Amanda Gorman*

The connection - Love is yours.
If you dive into the concept of self-love, invest time, and commit yourself bravely to it – there is a high chance that Love will be yours. It is the beginning of a life-long romance. It bridges everything. From cultivating a deep sense of self-worth, letting go of the past, enjoying your appearance, accepting our shadows to taking radical responsibility for ourselves and looking after ourselves.

The spectrum of self-love is wide and quite intimate, and you can find a lot of support from books, methods, classes, or diverse humans who cross your path. We have varied "selves" within. Which means in some roles or parts of life you will be able to love and accept yourself easily.

Let me give you an example: A woman who is competent and successful in her job, loves and accepts herself extensively in this respect. However, due to the double burden and the scarce time she spends with her children, she often doubts whether she is a good mother. Therefore, she lacks the love for herself in her role as a mother.

Instead of going into an inner battle, she can now approach her issue as a mother with the qualities she loves about herself as a businesswoman. For example, by structuring her time at home, taking notes on what is going well in her role as a mother, or asking for feedback from others. In a way, she is feeding her beloved part with the not so loved part of herself to achieve inner peace and to get the love and recognition she deserves as a mother.

Gratitude is another tool that can strengthen your self-love without much effort, but with enormous depth. This can be done very simply with a gratitude journal, in which you write 3 things every evening for which you are grateful. Or a prayer of gratitude that you say in the morning. You can include the areas where you have difficulty loving and accepting yourself.

A common theme, for example, is self-love in relation to our bodies. Instead of seeing our body as a gift, many women focus on perceived flaws that are subject to society's idea of beauty. The fact is, our body is a miracle of nature in which countless physiological processes run in parallel every single moment. Instead of trying too hard to love how your body looks, start making a gratitude ritual focused on the functions of your body. Gratitude for functioning organs, legs that carry you, skin that protects you, or simply for our beautiful beating heart that keeps us alive.

Please take a few deep breaths in and out. Be aware of your beautiful self in this beautiful moment. With every breath open your heart wider than you have ever opened it before. Let universal love generously flow in, for your life, your uniqueness, your goddess part, the love to share with others and for the wonderful person who is with you from the very beginning to the end - all your life. Yourself.

Tanja Stephanie Rug – Intuitive Coach

What is happiness?

Most of us spend our lives searching for happiness. Looking to experience more of that, and less of the not so comfortable stuff. All our lives we are told what happiness looks like, whether that is from advertisements, films, storybooks or even from our own friends and family. Our view and perception of happiness is shaped by the lives we live. Often, we can overlook or ignore a deep knowing whether something is making us happy or not, because of what we feel 'should' make us happy.

Have you ever had a time in your life when you really wanted something because everyone else seemed to have it? Perhaps the latest gadget, tickets to a concert or those trendy new trainers. Only to find out that when you actually get them you feel a little underwhelmed, or massively underwhelmed in my experience. It doesn't make sense though, right? Because everyone else looked so happy once they had that 'thing'. What that tells me is that happiness is personal to you. Only you truly know inside you what brings you happiness. That is the thing, it all happens *inside* of you.

I understand that some material items may bring you feelings of happiness. When you go to pick your new car up or buy that dream house that you worked so hard for. But the feelings; they all are inside of you and in my experience, they never last for long. Even then two different people could be gifted a brand-new sports car and one can be extremely happy and the other not so much. How? Because it is our own personal perception of the world that shapes us and our experiences.

Here is the thing that not many people will tell you: none of us need the sports car and dream house to help us experience happiness. Everything you have to feel and experience even more happiness, is already within you right now.

Close your eyes for one moment and think about something that you associate with being happy. It could be laughter on a loved one's face, that feeling when you sink into a deep bubble bath, or how it feels to kick your shoes off as you walk through the door after a very long shift at work. Even here now in this moment you can start to create those feelings of happiness. It is all within you.

Today I understand that happiness lies within me. But it has not always been this way. I spent a chunk of my life unhappy, thinking my actions would lead me to happiness. But the truth is they lead me down a one-way street to misery.

Have you ever had a time in your life where you felt strongly that you were here on this planet to make a positive difference? Well for me, as long as I can remember I have had this inner desire to spread kindness and smiles. And to help others to enjoy this journey here on earth. I could feel it in every cell in my body. I was put on this earth to serve others and create a positive impact. When you have a desire and passion that strong, it becomes difficult not to take action aligned to it.

The thing was, I got it all wrong. I wanted to make others smile and be happy. So, I 'fixed' their problems for them. Can you imagine how much energy that takes? I was available for people to lean on 24/7. I had no boundaries. I would just continue giving to others, no matter what time of day it was. I ignored my own needs. Yes, I felt wiped out and drained, but I ignored that as I felt I had a duty to make sure everyone else was happy. The word "NO" did not exist in my vocabulary. Whatever it is that you needed doing I would say "yes". I ignored my intuition.

Here is the big one – all this was making me miserable. My mission to make others happy lead me to be unhappy.

On reflection it seems obvious now why I was unhappy. Reading this I am sure that you can imagine how quickly I must have burnt out. Perhaps you recognise some of those behaviours in yourself, and it is impacting how you feel right now.

So, what changed? Well, you guessed it I burnt out. I almost lost everything I care most about in this world. A camel can only carry so much straw for so long, right? I was piling everyone else's straw on my back and had been for far too long.

Something had to change. Drastically.

I stopped. For the first time in my life. I embraced stillness and silence. They are natural and important for us, but prior to this moment I had purposely kept busy to avoid how I felt when things were still and silent. There is no hiding from your feelings in those quiet, still moments.

This time it was different. I knew exactly what I needed to do. I had to reconnect with myself. Be in my own energy, face whatever came up and deal with it. As humans we are fundamentally motivated to make changes either by pain or pleasure. For me It was pain. I had got to a point where I no longer recognised my own needs, I was unhappy, and I was living my life for everyone else, not myself.

I had to really go inwards and learn to be gentle with myself. Access every area of my life and start taking action to look after me, to protect my energy and get back in touch with my own happiness. It meant being really honest with myself, treating myself with compassion and practicing self-love. I took one day at a time and asked myself some pretty big questions every day like "What will lead me to feel good today?". I had spent so long being everything to everyone else, it was not easy to choose me.

I started meditating to become comfortable with the stillness and silence I had avoided for far too long. It helped me become familiar with myself, my intuition, and my needs. It took some time to get comfortable with understanding those needs, saying "No" and ultimately it cost me some relationships. There were times the people pleaser inside me was screaming to be let loose. It took patience, compassion, and gentleness to just be with myself.

Once I understood on a deeper level that I was in charge of my own happiness, and I already had everything I needed to experience happiness my life totally transformed. It is difficult for me to put into words how this one thing literally changed my life.

It is never easy doing the inner work. What made it more difficult for me was that I had no one to guide me. I did not know anyone who had a similar experience, I did not have any friends who I could speak to about this stuff.

I fumbled about for a while, reading as many books on happiness, self-care, and growth as I could get my hands on. I went hard on my own personal and spiritual development and completely transformed my life. One of the main reasons I now help others to do the same today is because I would have really benefited from support and encouragement on my own journey of self-discovery.

Today I use all my own experience, my knowledge and qualifications and support others on their own journey to experiencing more happiness. Helping them discover what happiness looks and feels like to them. Then taking action to create some space for more of that in their lives.

If you can relate to my struggles with happiness, I invite you to be really open minded and open hearted while you explore each area of your life. Allow yourself to be vulnerable with yourself. Keep a bucket load of compassion, love, and acceptance on standby and put all judgements in the bin. Trust that wherever your journey is taking you, you are right where you need to be at this moment. I believe you were guided to read this for a reason. There is something you can take from my experience with you on the next part of your journey.

The truth is we never need to search for happiness, it's right there within you waiting to be experienced. Welcome it. Enjoy it. Embrace it!

Helen Bartram – Happiness Coach

As a Divine Goddess, Spiritual gifts are part of your innate being.

As a divine goddess gifts are an innate part of your being. Your beautiful soul may have silenced some aspects of your personality for personal reasons. Like peer pressure, environment growing up, logic, or temperament. However dormant these gifts may be, they remain, ever ready to be acknowledged and strengthened.

Every goddess (that is you!) is born with six senses: sight, sound, touch, taste, smell and intuition. Your sixth sense is that extra sensory perception of your other senses. This is where your gut feeling, and inner knowingness resides. This is *your* superpower as a divine goddess.

I know you are already familiar with your intuition. (It is why you picked up this book and knew you needed it!) Your intuition is also the key to unlocking your spiritual lifestyle. It helps you connect with crystals, manifest with sacred geometry, and not only connect, but work you with your spirit guides!

Working with spirit guides is like pressing the *easy* button in life. Angels help resolve issues, provide encouragement and guidance. Fairies help with learning and utilizing spiritual tools. And what goddess would not have a Power Animal to help champion her through life's current path?

Your divine inner Goddess knows there is something more to life. Like that sense when you are trying to pull in a memory and it seems to be at the tip of your tongue...

Struggling with a decision, or life in general has become the acceptable norm and yet, you know it is not supposed to be that way. Especially when there are angels, ascended masters, power animals, and fairies just waiting to help! They are on standby! Ready to be called in at a moment's notice.

When you think about a situation, you have probably already considered the signs that, in hindsight, were present. Maybe you had a feeling, heard a repeated message, or saw a feather. Something kept trying to get your attention, but you did not realise. At this point you have a fork in the road type of moment.

Do I follow or do I ignore? It is your choice!

So how do you know it is your intuition?

How do you know it is an angel, a fairy, or another spirit guide, and not your imagination?

How do you confidently return and take action in this seemingly magical world that you have not visited since you were a little girl?

Here are 3 Keys to unlocking the magical realm:

1 - RECONNECT WITH YOUR INTUITION

Your intuition is your divine guidance system. Identify your personal intuitive preference.

Intuitive Sight – Seeing physical signs, objects, messages, and auras. This would be noticing a symbol (like a rainbow) or sign in your mind's eye; seeing an actual feather or coin on the ground or nearby; or seeing a series of numbers. You intuitively see the message from your spirit guides. (This is beneficial in working with all spirit guides – especially fairies)

Intuitive Sound – Hearing a message in a song, a sound or a conversation (although no one may even be there). Hearing a thought that seems to come out of nowhere. (This is extremely beneficial when working with all spirit guides!)

Intuitive Touch – Touching an object and getting insight regarding it. Feeling goosebumps, warmth or coolness, a tingling sensation or spark of energy. (This is extremely beneficial in working with crystals)

Intuitive Taste – Experiencing the sensation of a flavor in your mouth. Often a sweet or sour flavor, a coppery taste, exotic spice, or bitter taste. This gives insight as to herbs, favourite dishes, or communicates ailments and suggested solutions.

Intuitive Smell – Smelling a scent literally out of the air. A sudden whiff of flowers, a rainy day, a snowy morn, a day at the beach, a favourite perfume, wet fur, tobacco, fresh lit candle, smokey bonfire, fresh paint. Our nose can sniff danger! Able to smell emotions that linger in a room, intuitive smell has saved lives (Something does not smell right! Let's get out of here!) This also connects with memories and cherished moments. Beneficial when working with aromatherapy, this is also extremely advantageous when working with Power Animals, Mermaids and Fairies.)

Intuitive knowingness – Knowing the answer. A clear and yet unexplained of having the solution, the response, or interpretation of messages from spirit guides.

Intuitive feeling – Instinctually reacting. Having a gut feeling. You cannot explain it, you just sense it. Often this is "Mother's Intuition." Power Animals and Fairies boost this intuitive voice.

2 - YOUR GODDESS PERSONALITY

Each goddess personality lends itself to an intuitive preference. Ideally, grow, trust, and take action on all of your intuitive senses. Your goddess will naturally start out with one of the senses already hypersensitive!

Goddess of Action – naturally responds with her intuitive feeling. This enables her to make immediate decision.

Goddess of Order – naturally responds with her intuitive hearing. Able to hear the words and read between the lines of any messages. This goddess hears the messages of all the spirit guides, just needs to trust.

Goddess of Optimism – naturally responds with her intuitive sight. While many tease that this goddess has a short attention span, it is this personality strength that enables her to be distracted by the flash of light of a fairy zipping by, or the opalescent orb of an angel.

Goddess of Peace – naturally responds with intuitive feeling. Truly compassionate, she steps into another's shoes as best as she can. She picks up the subtle energies in the air, in a voice, in an aura. She will feel the ache or pain within her own body. She will also just have an unexplained feeling of knowingness.

By working with fairies, every goddess personality will be able to connect and strengthen each intuitive voice! Fairies used to mentor us whenever it came to things of this world like farming, nature, herbs, cooking, creating, healing, and intuition.

By working with fairies, you will find more confidence in your intuition and messages, and step into taking action aligned with your divine goddess!

3 - WORK WITH FAIRIES

Identify your goddess personality.

Take the goddess quiz – www.trishmckinnley.com/goddess to discover your natural goddess personality. You may find that you are a blend of two, or three or that only one stands out. There is no wrong or right personality. You are divinely and perfectly made, from stardust, and truly meant to shine.

Knowing your goddess personality helps you communicate with other goddesses, the universe, and your spirit guides, as you manifest your dreams into reality

Every goddess personality can work with *every* spirit guide. Just like your goddess temperament lends itself to naturally aligning with particular intuitive insight, it also easily connects with various spirits guides.

In this section learn which spirit guide each goddess connects with and how to connect with fairies.

Goddess of Action naturally aligns with dragon energy - (able to be grounded, take charge, and see things through). There are fairy dragons to connect with. This will enable her to keep her power under control, while remaining open to team suggestions and creating a unified message.

The Goddess of Action working with dragon fairies.

Go outdoors in nature for a walk or run. Before you start, request fairies to connect with you. "Fairies, fairies, come to me. With humbleness and admiration, your connection I seek."

As you state these words, imagine a ray of pink light shining from your heart chakra. Imagine this light illuminating your path and being a welcome sign for the right fairy connection. As you venture on your walk/run be observant to any signs, thoughts and impressions fairy give you! You may hear rustling in leaves and there is no wind. You may see a black "insect" and yet felt something was different.

Whenever you receive an intuitive insight thank the fairies aloud. At that time, you can begin discussing a project or area where you would like assistance. If you want to build the relationship more, ask fairies to meet you here again. Continue the process of inviting, meeting, talking, and thanking.

Building a relationship with fairies is like all relationships. Trust. Patience and respect. Once you have established your foundation with fairies, they will assist you in your projects and endeavors. (Even if it is getting your kids in bed at a decent time!)

Goddess of Order works well with mermaids. It is an easy transition for her to work with fairies. This goddess benefits from a relationship with fairies because they help dispel any insecurities and increase her trust in her own knowingness. Logic and perfectionism are often this goddess's angst. Fairies provide the love and support and the quiet steps she needs, so she builds her confidence and stops overthinking.

To connect with fairies, write a short story or a poem about fairies. Create the plot around your first meeting. Fill in details of what it was like – the magic, joy, and appreciation. Conclude with how this was just the beginning of long, true friendship!

Once written, go outdoors near a flower garden, gorgeous tree or anywhere your intuition guides you. Read your story or poem aloud. Sense any messages. Fairies will often provide a full thought. Continue your writing and storytelling to continue building the relationship. This would be great to keep in a journal. You can add any intuitive messages, experiences, and inspiration.

When comfortable ask fairies for guidance! While they especially love working with gardens, fairies will gladly help bring more joy to a situation or alleviate overanalyzing any situation!

Goddess of Optimism works well with fairies. She is able to connect with the joy and keep her light shining bright. This goddess brightens a room when she walks in. Fairies help her heart chakra be protected and active. They help her stay focused when she ventures way off course, and they help her feel loved and valuable.

To connect with fairies, find a place to sing, dance and laugh. Fairies are naturally attracted to the joy. It does not matter what you wear. It does not matter what you sing, (make up a song about fairies to the tune of Happy Birthday!) Most importantly, let your arms swing out as if opening to the fairies in joy and love. Let them feel your sincere desire to connect with them! If you are feeling silly – even better. The joy will be a strong magnet calling to them.

If possible, journal what you experience. Do some songs bring more fairy interaction than others? Do they prefer music with your singing or just acapella? Did laughing and smiling seem easier when fairies were nearby? Ask fairies if there is an instrument they would like to hear! Keep the fairy friendship building!

Goddess of Peace works well with angels. Subtle and loving, kind and never pushy, this goddess works well with fairies for releasing the negative energy she unfortunately picks up. Often not her fault and not her drama. As a humanitarian and mediator, this goddess benefits from fairies' brilliance for creating the peaceful environment for all.

To work with fairies - cloud gaze! Whenever you venture outside, look skyward. Fairies will make shapes out of the clouds. You may notice unique shapes in leaves, branches, flower petals and stones. Look for the signs. What message are you picking up? Fairies often provide hearts. If you are given a stone or leaf on the ground in the shape, thank the fairies and pick it up. Place in your sacred space or another safe, cherished location.

Every time you notice your gift from the fairies thank them and reminiscence of the day by sharing the story aloud. Speak your appreciation.

Whenever working with fairies thank them. They are risking working with you. You are building a bridge that has been burnt by our ancestors. The more we help heal the relationship the better this whole world becomes!

One way to thank the fairies is to leave a tiny bowl of fresh water out every night. Place in a safe place.

While meditating, ask fairies what you can do to show them love and appreciation. Trust your intuition for the guidance you hear, see, feel, or know.

Have a picnic or celebration with them on their best times – the between times – dusk till dawn, with honey, milk, sweet breads, flowers, sparkles, and a proper tea.

Recognizing your divine goddess personality, identifying, growing your intuitive voice, and opening to a relationship with fairies will unlock and open the door to releasing your sacred goddess powers.

Trish McKinnley – Spiritual Lifestyle Expert

Becoming the Goddess of wealth creation.

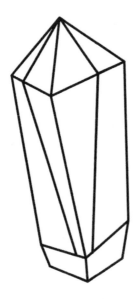

To be a star, you must shine your own light, follow your own path, and do not worry about darkness, for that is when the stars shine brightest –
Napoleon Hill

From being born poor in Sydney Australia, a middle child, a girl with two migrant European parents who never spoke a word of English; attending a poor school where I experienced racial abuse; to a woman building a Billion Dollar empire.
How did that happen?

As a young child I did not have much, but I did have a love of reading. The library became my refuge. Somewhere I could escape to. I treasured mystery books; stories about ghosts and goblins were another favourite. I used my imagination to escape the violence of my everyday life, and also to affirm that someday, no matter how, I was going to change the story of my life.

I also loved music and would dance on an imaginary stage in my backyard. There was no money for music, so imagine how happy I was when my Uncle bought me my first Abba album as a Christmas present. One song left a huge impression on me, and years later as a survivor of domestic violence and an unhappy marriage, the song "Money, money, money" would forever influence my decision to change my future.

Somewhere deep down, call it fate, call it destiny, a little girl made the decision to BE all she could be. In one of my favourite movies, Wizard of Oz, Dorothy was trying to find her way home back to Kansas. After all her adventures, Glinda, the good witch tells her:

"My dear, you always had the power, you just had to learn it for yourself."

Dorothy needed to learn to believe.

My marriage broke down when I was 30 years old. With two small children under the age of two I spent the next twenty years bringing them up, keeping my dream of being a billionaire hidden, even though deep down I knew it was written into my heart and soul.

As mothers and women, we are natural born leaders and project managers. Yes, you heard right. Bringing up children requires leadership skills, time management and budgeting skills, really project management 101!

At the ripe age of 47 I started working in IT. At the bottom of the ladder, working as a project co-ordinator on an extremely basic wage. After working solidly for 4 months, I was given a small rise, $2 in fact, and told, I was lucky to have that. I was so angry that day, I promised myself I would do everything it took to learn my job inside out. I started using positivity and manifestation techniques and it took me four months. When it came time to have my contract renewed, I told my boss what I thought I was worth. He agreed and told me "now you know how to play the game".

It was then I realised if your desire to be wealthy is strong enough, you will do whatever it takes. Upskill yourself, learn, hire coaches. If you do not know something, hire the best you can afford and most of all remember that YOU ARE YOUR OWN PR COMPANY. No-one knows you better than you. You know your own heart, passion, and dreams. Most of all you know what you truly are capable of, and how brightly that internal fire burns within you!

To be truly rich, wealthy beyond one's dreams, you must firstly understand that the negative self-talk, self-sabotage, all the stories we tell ourselves about money. Money is bad; Money does not equal happiness; I am not worthy.
All this is absolutely 100% BS.

I want to dive in, I do not want to waste a second of your time, with what money is not, I will tell you what money is and what money brings.

Money can give you a greater sense of freedom and power. With money you can travel, explore different cultures, learn, enjoy activities, help the impoverished and so much more.

If you are not happy with your current financial circumstances, no matter what age, colour, or gender you are. If you cannot get a job, think big then bigger and **become your own boss**.

You may say that you have to provide for your family or pay the rent. I completely understand. Do what you have to do, take a job any job and then invest in yourself. Put extra effort and hours into becoming your own boss and invest in you! YOU ARE WORTH IT AND SO MUCH MORE.

Goddesses you are the source, you are the gift, you are the power, look within, you need to get out of your way. I am also talking about silencing your mind chatter, outing all your fears, and being who you were meant to be.

As Josh Dawson, Director of Cardone Ventures said to me, "Ladies you need to find your "WHY". Your why is your passion and purpose, it is also making sure your dream is absolutely big enough. Your dream needs to be MEGA. It needs to wake you, and shake you to your core."

My dream and reality are I am a Billionaire, and I am building a Billion Dollar Empire!

Ask yourself this question: *Why could this not be your dream and reality?*

Ask yourself: *Can I really be a Billionaire?*

Just for a minute dream that this is your reality, how does it feel?

My Mantra is:
"If the mountain will not come to Muhammad, then Muhammad must go to the Mountain."

You must do whatever it takes. **Become unstoppable**. As a woman Building a Billion Dollar empire it is not all sunshine and roses. You will lose friends, some people will not like that you are progressing to greatness.

This has nothing to do with you and should ignite your determination further. Do not dim your light to fit in, it serves no purpose. If anything, be inspired to shine even brighter.

Find like-minded ambitious people with heart and soul.

Find even more successful people to uplift you to greatness.

Find people who are not the people you would not normally hang with.

All this will create room for growth and new conversations.
Be aware of the level of your energy and enthusiasm in your business. Each of us operate at a different speed. Life is not "one speed suits all". As a Goddess of Wealth, I am able to manifest the right connections and people easily. I often refer myself to the Shinkansen (bullet train). Claim your speed as it is part of your source energy and power.

It does not mean that people who move slower cannot achieve mega wealth. It may just take them a bit longer to reach Wealth Mountain. But if you get up every day, stay motivated, do one big bold action towards your goal, you will get there.
You must truly understand that great wealth requires you to adopt a mindset of "**I am unstoppable**".

It is never too late to be who you are really meant to be. I am in my early 50's and on my way to being a Billionaire. Know that it is NEVER too late to achieve your dream.

Goddesses. I am asking you to embody being "unstoppable". This is more than higher vibration. It is about finding your WHY. You must turn on your own light, discover your passion and your purpose and find your **Mega Dream**.

Your dream should make you want to jump out of bed each and every single day. It needs to make you smile from ear to ear; and to bring you immense joy. Because with joy in your heart, your purpose and passion will make your wealth and business goals a reality.

I get up each and every day and my heart sings.

I kindly ask you to give gratitude and thanks to where you currently are in your life and acknowledge that you are perfection just as you are. You are an infinite bright light in this beautiful word and cosmos. There is only one of you. You are unique so you must get your message out to the world!!

For my part I know nothing with any certainty, but the sight of the stars makes me dream - Vincent Van Gogh

The methods I use are "Affirmative Prayer" and being in God Source. Yes Goddesses, I pray a lot, sometimes up to four hours a day. I am not asking you to do this level of prayer, however long time ago I heard "Big requests Big prayers!" For me it goes hand in hand. Affirmative prayer is a 5-step prayer process.

1. Recognising God as the source
2. Knowing that you are God (a smaller version)
3. Stating your intention to God/source of what you want. For example: God I am financially independent making a Billion dollars plus (that was my intention)
4. Giving thanks to God
5. Surrendering the prayer to God as being answered.

This is a what I believe has allowed me to have mega success. After being in prayer, I feel I am in "flow". I am given suggestions as whispers or ideas.

What else have I done?
- I visualise myself where I want to be.
- I say to myself every day, "I am going to make it."
- I have developed an "unstoppable" mindset.
- I have developed a mindset of great wealth is my birth right to take!
- I associate only with positive people and positive thoughts.
- I state my intentions through prayer with 2000% conviction.

Jasmin Baljak – Goddess of Wealth Creation

Fear only exists in mind.

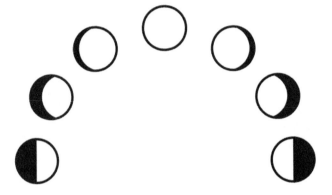

When I was 11 years old my Dad left. There you go. I am sure many of you can relate to this. I am not going to dwell on it, but it is key to my story, you need to know it. But there is no drama in this chapter about him leaving. I made my peace with that years ago.

Incredibly, my father's mobile number is still the only mobile number I can remember off the top of my head besides my own. Our relationship is the single most important one I have had to heal in order to become the woman I am today.

Now let's rewind...

My dad left the summer before I started secondary school, that's High School to those in the US. I vaguely remember Mr Castle, my teacher at the time, telling my mother I had an attitude problem, at my final parent's evening at primary school. My mother was distraught. I, on the other hand, had every intention of wearing that 'attitude' as a badge of honour.

That 'attitude' was my shield. It kept people at a distance, not a huge distance, because I needed connection and friendship. But the shield that was going to stop me ever again feeling the hurt I felt, the moment my dad shut the back gate and drove off in his burgundy ford Mondeo.

I should probably apologise to anyone that knew me at that time. Because I was not the best version of myself at that time. I pushed people away when they got close. Said hurtful things about others to cause drama, then slipped away. As an adult who has done the work, I can see that I did not do this for fun. I did it to stop anyone else leaving on their own terms.

I had created a fail-proof system of 'If I push you, you will leave before we get too attached'. It worked like a charm! Someone starts to become too close; you say something bad; they end the friendship and then it is onto the next person. Repeat cycle. We were children, don't forget.

I lost some good friends over the years, and I moved tutor groups twice. Because when it came down to it I could not cope with the flames of the fires I was lighting. There were times when I crumbled. When the little girl in me threatened to break through the harsh exterior I had created. Eventually she would fully break through, but that happened much later on.

As I got older, friendship brought me lessons of loss and love. When I was in college, I lost the first love of my life, and then I lost my best friend at the age of twenty-five. I am pretty sure they are both up there causing a great deal more havoc up there than I ever will down here. Although you never know...there is still plenty time for me to cause a lot more trouble!

Losing two of your closest friends at such a young age was a reminder that life can be fleeting, and that you should always show up in all your glory. I felt this lesson in my core, and for a while there was a lot of wine, and much bitterness about being 'left' by those I loved most.

When I became pregnant with my daughter, I had my first awakening. It was not full of angels and rainbows. It was more of a 'pull the rug from underneath you' kind of thing. More people left, there was a lot of anger and frustration, and of course there was a shit tonne of fear I could no longer avoid wading through.

People leave. As the old saying goes "People come into your life for a reason, a season or a lifetime" I could no longer live with a closed heart, pushing people away with my shield built of sarcasm and my sword of sharp-tongued replies. I had to change, not those around me. Me.

This is where the real work began.

I have never been one to sugar coat anything. But looking closely at myself, seeing my habits and patterns. I had a revelation. This shield-wielding maiden would need to put down her beloved shield completely to be able to fully explore this new world. I had dropped it a little over the past few years and my shoulders had begun to relax when I felt safe. But now I knew that to fully evolve I would have to put down the shield completely. The thought of this made me sick.

But I began to do the inner work and I quickly saw the answer to all of my roadblocks was fear. I was always running from fear and avoiding it by hiding behind my shield.

The realisation that fear only existed in my mind was the pivot in my life. And everything changed.

Let's talk about fear...

We have all experienced fear in our lives. It wakes us up at night, stops us from doing the things we want to do, and from sharing our true selves with the world. Oh yes, it all boils down to fear.

Fear was the fog that was blocking me from my true vision. Once I began to realise that, the fog lifted, and I could truly see this human experience for the magic that it is.

Did you know that human beings are only born with two fears? The fear of falling and the fear of loud noises. So, we can safely say that all of our other fears are brought on by perceptions, beliefs and the opinions of others.

So here I am with the facts. On the one hand fear does not exist. On the other fear is the product of a certain part of my brain. I was confused until I realised that combining true science and spirituality gave me the answer. Fear exists, but only in my mind.

As the years went by, my family began discussing that in this human experience we have two paths. One of fear and one of love. We are the first to yell 'Triggered!" across the kitchen when someone says something that upsets us. Then we will explore why that happened and how we can deal with that feeling.

We understand that all our emotions, and even our actions will fall into these two categories. It is such a simple fact that it is often overlooked. Am I acting out of fear? Or out of love? Are my words coming from a place of love or fear? Once you begin to question this, you will find the answer is always very clear.

So how can you tell the difference between fear and love?

I believe that fear controls and restricts; love accepts and flows. Fear divides and, my favourite one, love unites. Fear says: if you say how you really feel, then no one will love you; Tells you that you are better off saying nothing at all, because people love the ones that are quiet, right? Fear is lying. Fear suppresses your soul whereas love gives you the freedom to explore those parts of it that are still untamed.

Love to me feels still. Fear feels frantic. If you are being chased by a wild cat in the wilderness fear is useful. But in everyday life it is fear that blocks us from our goddess dreams of living an untamed life.

When you focus on love you see the oneness in others, you forgive more easily and you might just find you sleep more easily too.

How to overcome fear? Truth is, you cannot overcome something that does not exist. When we really break it down, we are not in fear every moment of our lives. To create fear, we have to use excessive amounts of imagination. You are creating things in your mind, in one thousand different formats that may not even happen.

Can we ever fully let go of fear? Probably not. Because it is part of each of us. If you want the science to back it up, fear is a sub nucleus of the amygdala part of the brain. It has a purpose, and it is not going anywhere. Fear is an essential part of us but we should not let it rule our lives.

One of the most important things I have learnt is that fear loses its power when you remove the idea of judgement. Also, fear cannot survive in the present tense. It can only survive in the past or in the future. Which for me meant I had to stop pushing people away. I needed to be present.

I have come to the realisation that fear always comes along for the ride. Fear will find you halfway up the mountain, it will whisper to you between the crashing waves. However, you are in control of your own mixed tape. You can choose the tunes that spark love in your heart and fire in your belly to keep moving forward.

Am I saying we should ignore your emotions? Definitely not, these feeling are often an indicator that there is inner work to be done. I am simply reminding you all. You have the final say on the songs you listen to and add to your playlist.

Fear is the fog that blocks our vision and when we see that the fog lifts and we can see this existence for the magical experience that it is. How can we remove the power fear has over us? Luckily for me, my reiki master and dear friend Yvonne Bottarelli provided me with the tools and now I am sharing them with you.

She explained to me once that one of the simplest ways to take control of your fear is to ask yourself "And then what?"

So, you fail an exam; "and then what?"
Then you will have to restudy and take it again; "and then what?"

You keep doing this until you get to the worst-case scenario.

This simple act exhausts the fear which then loses this imaginary hold you believed it had over you. By doing this you are emptying the engine of fear and draining it of its power.

We all feel afraid from time to time. But we let it drive us, not control us. We work from a place of open mind and open heart.

It took me a long time to see this pattern in my life. That when I was coming from a place of fear, I was not my best self. But the hardest lesson was seeing this in others. Understanding that when someone is coming from a place of fear, they need to be greeted with boundaries and love.

I invite you to take a walk with your fear. Ask it where it is really coming from. Befriend it, take it for a dance and really connect to it.

Does fear still exist in the world of Charlie?

Of course it does! Sometimes me and fear will dance, other times we will argue.

I am loud, I am fun and if you have ever had the joy of receiving an audio message from me you know I shoot from the hip. I live in the space of 'why not' and I am now in a space where I have no issue with fear being with me on this rodeo we call life.

In fact, I am aware that fear is with me right now as I write this chapter.

But let's just say that today we have come to an understanding... I write and she listens.

Oceans of Love

Charlie Edwards – Editor, Untamed Soul Magazine

The stories that keep us from our truth.

As I sit here, ready to start writing this chapter for you to read, I smile. I smile because, looking back at the life I have lived, the struggles that I went through, all because of the beliefs I had and my innocently not knowing any better than to believe and act from them.

It is almost unbelievable to me now, that I used these unfounded beliefs as my bible for life, a rulebook that would not let me grow. A way to stay and play small.

Now my life is just so different. I have moved on from not believing in myself; from constantly telling myself that I was not worthy, or capable, of doing well in life. That I was not clever enough, I was not bright enough. That I had no voice. Often asking myself why on earth would anyone want to listen to me. I had nothing worth sharing.

As I sit here now, today, I believe it is time to speak with my own true voice. I am excited to be sharing it with you, right here, right now, trusting that it is a message that deserves to be shared.

I grew up in a family where we were taught to shush, to be quiet. Told that what I had to say was not important. Adults matter more, you know nothing, we do not have time to listen to you.

Is it any wonder I decided to accept those messages repeated over and over as true?

Is it any wonder I created beliefs from those throw away comments?

Is it any wonder I believed nobody wanted to listen to me?

Now, I can see things from a different perspective. Now I see that being told to shush and the constant criticisms were never meant to have the long-lasting impact they ended up having.

It was me I gave them meaning and created a set of beliefs from them all.

It was me. Who decided and created an internal rule book from all those instructions on how to make my way in and through life? It was me who created a belief that I had no confidence.

I used to watch other people appear to glide through life with ease, grace, and good fortune. I used to ask myself; "How did they get so lucky? How was everything so easy for them? How did they just know they had something to say worth hearing?

The Julie growing up and for many of her adult years, is a completely different Julie than the one sitting writing this chapter.

The Julie sitting writing this chapter, telling her story, speaking up, is different in so many ways to that younger Julie.

No longer do I just go through the motions of life. No longer am I afraid to speak up, afraid to be seen and heard.

I was and still am creating the reality I live in. I get to choose the life I live. I get to decide. I am able to step up like a woman from a TV advert, hair flowing in the wind, standing proud and declaring THIS IS ME.

I no longer believe that life just happened to me. That road only leads to a life of disempowerment, a life of disappointment, a life of hurt and blame. I no longer live in victim mode.

I am no victim.

I am a strong, worthy powerful woman. Just like YOU.

The world is here to support me, to help me grow, fly, and live an abundant life from love. Love for myself and others.

The world is here to support you, to help you grow, to fly and to live an abundant life from love. It is time to love yourself.

From all the experiences I have had in my life, I have learned many lessons. My wisdom has tapped me on the shoulder many times. When I did not listen the first time, it always came back, stubbornly, tapping again. It is always there supporting me.

So, you might be wondering what changed? How did I go from a quiet, shy, girl, then a woman with low self-esteem and little confidence, to the proud, confident woman I am now? And how is my life different in that reality?

Well, I am in a happy marriage, for over 17 years and while there have been ups and downs, some pretty big, I am confident enough in myself to know I can get through anything that comes my way in life.

I woke up!

I woke up and understood I can live any life I choose.

I woke up and understood EVERY SINGLE ONE OF US has a message worth hearing.

I woke up and understood I am more powerful than I have ever given myself credit for.

I woke up to who I truly am.

Then I took action with my new knowledge guiding me forward.

I now have two wonderful daughters and have accepted the loss of my son and know he will always be by my side and in my life.

I have a thriving business, even though we are in the middle of a worldwide pandemic and are in and out of local and national lockdowns, my business has grown to the best it has ever been.

I know no matter what restrictions or obstacles that come my way, I will always be free. I will always be okay. I can deal with any situation that arises. I can still live the life I choose and share my message with the world. I have got this.

You see life has a way of ebbing and flowing. There will always be ups and downs. But just like a river always finds the best path to flow, will naturally be guided to the best path for our flow.

So now instead of being that shy, quiet girl who did not want to speak up. Or the defensive women who always felt like she had to defend herself, explain herself, or live up to beliefs of her own making, I can trust the natural flow of my life has my heart at its core. I follow the wisdom of the river; I live in the ebb and flow of life.

I am capable of achieving everything I want to achieve. I know there is an abundance of everything in life available to me. We do not need to be afraid of things running out, there is always enough. We can just get up and live our life, in our own unique imperfectly perfect way in every way, every day.

You see that is what living is, it is not going through the motions. It is not trying to live up to the expectations of others. It is not believing the limiting beliefs we impose on each other. It is not being the person that we believe we have to be. It is not reliving our past, reliving the events that we have blamed for us not being able to have the life we want.

I can create the life I want.

You can create the life you want. Anytime we want, all we have to do is to take the actions that start and move that creation forward.

If you are reading this and are sitting thinking to yourself "Yeah right! Of course, it is as easy as you say". I have a question for you to ask yourself.

What is actually stopping you?

What is stopping you from taking one small action towards a life that you want? One small action.

In the UK we are in lockdown as I write this., We have been in and out of it most of the year. We cannot go out, and there are so many restrictions that seem to change from week to week and yet, I am still as free as I have always been. Our freedom comes from our minds. We get to choose to live the life that is our birth right. We get to choose to live it as fully as possible.

We are only on this planet in this form for a short length of time in the grand scheme of things. So why the heck not live it to its full potential. Why the heck not enjoy, experience and relish every single part of it.

Often the things that we experience, that we label as something we do not like, will have lessons for us to learn in them somewhere. In the same way that things we experience that we label as things we enjoy will help us learn too.

Our lives are crammed full of experiences that we label as "our life" and yet they are not wholly our life. They are all individual parts that we bundle together and blend in our minds to make "our life".

There will always be something to make meaning of, there will always be lessons to learn, always something that will spark some hope for change in our future. But we have to embody the spark, take action, and engage with forward movement. Focusing on our worry and our stress, and then expecting our lives to get better never works. Focusing on what we can do, taking action, and believing in the amazingness of ourselves is what changes lives.

We choose the life we want, and we get it by how we act. When we see that life is filled with abundance, that it flows forever, that we can have anything we set our heart and intention on, then we can start moving in the right direction to claim and live it as ours.

When we stop living like a victim of life, believing that life just happens to us and that it can never get any better, we start seeing new possibilities, wider horizons, and abundant opportunities in every aspect of our life.

When we say YES to all of the above and YES to life then the universe hears us and says YES back.

Right now, as I am writing this chapter for this book, I have had those old habitual thoughts pop up again. Asking why am I doing this? Why would anyone want to listen to me? But that is okay. I know those thoughts are options, that I can choose to listen to or ignore. What does it look like I chose to do with them?

So now it is time to share this with you and to ask YOU, what actions will you take that will propel you forward?

What steps can you take to fully embody the true goddess in you?

I suggest you start with some self-love.

Without fully accepting that you are a perfectly imperfect goddess you will continue to judge yourself.

By owning and loving yourself you will allow those judgments to drift away as you engage with the life you were born to live.

Where your focus goes, your experience shows. So, check in often with yourself.

- What are you currently seeing?
- What else is there to see?
- How are you interacting with yourself?
- What can you do that would bring a different outcome?

I invite you to journal often on these questions and become the expert in, and on, you and how to allow the best of you to shine brightly.

Remember no mountain was climbed in one stride, it takes many smaller, easier steps to reach the top. Believe in yourself, take one step at a time, love and appreciate your mind and your body. You only get one of each, and they are serving you as best they can. Are you serving them?

Take action!

Remember you always get to choose.

No matter what, you have got this because YOU are a powerful goddess.

Much love xx

Julie Brown – Women's Empowerment Expert

Rising into self-acceptance.

I sat at my kitchen table, with tears rolling down my face and realised that something had to change. I felt so helpless. I had no idea what to do or where to turn next. Struggling to cope with the demands of everyday life. I had been trying to 'be' and 'do' everything for everyone else. To be the perfect mum, the perfect wife, be successful in my career, be a great friend and be the one who went around visiting all the family.

The truth is I was exhausted and burnt out. I had everything I could have wished for. Except one thing, my self-worth.

Having reached the ceiling point in my career, after 7 years, I felt ready to progress to the next level. I was appointed to a new role, but a challenging interaction with a senior manager created a 'tipping' point for me. bringing a whole host of personal challenges and creating cycles of self-sabotage which were underpinned by all the negative beliefs which were simmering away underneath.

It took someone else to point out that I was running on adrenaline, in a constant state of stress. I could not see it for myself. This was the turning point, the point where I knew I had to start rebuilding, take my power back and start looking after myself.

My lack of self-worth had manifested into a challenging relationship with food. From binging, purging, and taking laxatives as a teenager, to using food to comfort and numb me and help me ignore my feelings. I was lonely but did not realise it. I was also disconnected from my body, after experiencing sexual trauma. This led to me shutting off my emotions which often happens in that situation. Controlling what I ate was a great coping mechanism.

Constantly on the go, keeping busy 24/7, meant I never stopped and listened to my body. I became addicted to the feeling of being permanently in a stress-response state and actively worked to maintain my stress levels. My husband once said to me "You just replace one stress in your life with another".

That was a stark realisation for me. This contributed to my continued struggles with my weight. I was stress eating, eating high sugar food throughout the day in response to my stress at work. During a stress response the blood chemistry is affected in such a way that It can lead to increased fat stores around the mid-section.

My confidence was closely linked to my weight. Feeling that I could not progress in my career because I did not feel good about myself. I pushed myself to achieve, collecting certificates to show prove that I was worthy. In my head, my identity was linked to my achievements at work. Without them, I had no idea who 'Sarah' was. I did not even know my own voice.

The truth is I was unhappy. The word 'joy' felt alien to me, I did not know how to experience that feeling, it was a word that I could not describe. The only thing that brought me something close to joy was food. The phrase "what are we going to eat next" consumed my thoughts every hour of every day.

Despite everything I was going through, and the stories I was telling myself, deep down I always felt like I was meant for more. That yearning feeling kept driving me forward and had me striving for something better.

As a mum I never allowed any time for myself. I felt guilty if I did anything for 'me'. Trying to be there for everyone else, dealing with everyone else's problems made me feel needed and therefore worthy. I had always struggled with the word 'NO' and I had no personal boundaries. This came from a fear of rejection and not being liked.

Taking on more work, saying yes to everything, but then feeling resentful or disappointed with myself as it was not what I wanted. Always too scared to be on my own so jumping from one relationship straight into another. I am ashamed to say it, but I seemed to be attracted to drama.

Someone told me "Sarah, you are always so negative". That comment felt like a punch in the gut. At the time I was hurt and upset. But now I realise it was a great gift. I had no self-awareness, and this comment was an eye opener, bringing an awareness of how I was projecting.

I had created stories in my own head about not feeling good enough. I had a belief that I sounded thick because of my accent. I was too scared to speak up or make a mistake afraid of being embarrassed or judged, I felt I was not being heard, that I did not have a voice.

Things are different now. My journey of self-discovery has brought me insight and self-awareness of my relationships with myself, other people. And with food!

Food and body peace
By exploring my stories and beliefs around my body and food, I have learned to slow down and let go of my judgements around food. I no longer view food as good or bad. I have let go of the diet mentality, calorie counting and any restrictions.
Now I focus on how I can nourish my body with high quality foods. I listen to my body and notice the feelings that are triggering or driving my behaviours with food without listening to my inner critic.

After having 2 babies via C-section, I found it hard to love my body. But I have moved to a place of body peace and self-compassion. We cannot hate ourselves into weight loss. This creates stress and puts our body into that stress response. When we are eating, it is important that we make it a relaxing and enjoyable experience so that we are allow our bodies to relax which aids digestion and assimilation.

Self
Putting my own oxygen mask on first, remembering to value myself, taking time for me. Whether for meditation, or for treating myself in a way that fills my cup. I want to set a good example so that my kids learn to value themselves. Now they ask to listen to mediation themselves every night before bed.
I have learned to recognise my feelings, and the thought patterns and underlying beliefs that are creating them. I try to get out of my own head and start to feel into my body, listening and noticing the signs. If you make a decision and you get that feeling in the pit of your stomach, it is a sign that your decisions are not aligned.

Our beliefs create our thoughts, which creates our feelings and emotions, and our feelings and emotions create the behaviours that play out in our lives. Our lives are a reflection of what is going on inside. Our thoughts create our reality, the good the bad and the ugly. Now, when I am feeling anxious, or worried about something, rather than spiralling, I feel into the emotions and look for what the learning is. I can step back to question and review it with a different perspective. I look at the stories I am telling myself and ask; is that my truth?

Observe and start to notice the stories you play on repeat in your own head and start to question them. Where does the belief come from?
I am not a morning person...
I am not good at...
I will never be slim.
People like us are not...

Others
In relationships now I am able to step back and see other people's behaviour as a reflection of what is going on for them. I do not take things personally anymore and am able to navigate and facilitate discussions with a different perspective. I do not get drawn in and 'react' to situations.

I have put personal boundaries in place and recognise that my 'need' to listen to other people's drama was about *me* feeling worthy and needed. I have stepped back from engaging in those conversations. Before you say yes to anything, it is ok to say; 'can I think about it and get back to you?' This gives you time to think about what you really want.

I feel a deep sense of inner peace. I see every experience as an opportunity to grow. My perspective now is one of gratitude for all the experiences of my own journey. By understanding my own values and what is truly important to me I can make decisions which are aligned with those values.

What is important to you? Consider if you are living in alignment with your values. Discovering my true passions, my purpose, and my strengths, has allowed me to get back on course. I am closer to living the life of my dreams. Our purpose is related to the challenges we overcome in life.

Recognise your triumphs and consider how can you use them to help others.

I knew that I needed to figure out who 'Sarah' was.

I started by working with a mindset coach to help me through my breakdown. I learned to carve out some time for myself and started to take my power back. Every day on the school run I started a gratitude practice with my kids. We would take it in turns to share all the things we felt grateful for. I learned to change my state and found a "power' song". From The Greatest Showman, the song "This is me". With it blaring out the kids and I would be singing and dancing at the top of our voices. It helped to raise my vibration, my energetic and emotional state.
We have the power within us to create darkness or light. The challenge is to view your journey, and every experience, as a gift and not a curse. From the darkness comes the light. Reflect on your own experiences and look for your wisdom.

I started to dream about a life by the sea. I grew up in Port Talbot, South Wales and felt drawn to return, but we were living in London and I also liked city life and what it offered. Incredibly an opportunity to move to Sydney came up, and we grabbed it with both hands.

I have never been afraid to step out of my comfort zone. I was the first person in my family to move away, to go to university. I moved to America when I was 21. Now I was moving to the other side of the world with my young family. Leaving the comfort and safety of a secure job and my support network of family and friends. But the rewards could be amazing.

Start to paint a picture in your mind of the life you want to create. Then visualise it every day. "You only live once!" is a mantra that has been prominent in my life. Take time to figure out your own passions, find your purpose and create a fulfilling life.

After moving to Australia, I really began to reflect on my life and discover what excited me. I had a MSc in Nutrition, physical activity, and public health but I had ended up in a job that was completely unaligned with my values, beliefs, and passions.

Getting my own coaching qualification in eating psychology taught me how to slow down and find joy in my life. I used those moments of joy to change my state. I learned to recognise how stress impacted my life; learned strategies to deal with stress and let go of the yo-yo diets. I started healing my relationship with food. Began focusing on eating good quality, satisfying foods. Paying attention to my inner dialogue around food and my body. Now I feel at peace with my body.

"How can I nourish my mind, body and soul?" - a simple but very powerful question.

I have learned to recognise feelings within my body and how they are impacted by my own thoughts and beliefs. My trauma work has allowed me to heal experiences from the past allowing me to get to the root of my limiting beliefs.

My biggest realisation was that my fear of not being heard, not feeling that I had a voice and being too scared to express myself, was linked to a fear of judgement. I am working on having the courage to stand up and use my voice, to be heard! We are all responsible for our own beliefs.

Do not be afraid to examine your own thoughts and beliefs and question whether they are your truth.

Next steps
- Start to notice and appreciate the moments that bring you joy.
- Find your own power/feel good song!
- Reflect on how you can nourish yourself and what nourishment means to you. Consider how you can nourish you mind, body and soul.
- Slow down with food and life!
- Look for where you can improve the quality of food you eat and let go of the diet mentality-
- Bring awareness to your inner dialogue. What are the stories you have on repeat?
- Seek help to do your own trauma work. Explore small traumas from childhood which created a belief and you have carried that belief with you throughout your life.
- Explore your true passions and purpose in life.

If you feel like you are meant for more but have been feeling stuck in your life, then reach out. I help women fulfil their true potential and to live a life of true passion and purpose by uncovering their limiting stories and beliefs.

I wish you joy on your journey.

Sarah Battle – Spiritual Practitioner.

Share your voice.

Here we are. The last chapter of a book full of divine inspiration and loving encouragement. Each Goddess has opened her heart and shared something unique and beautiful, a precious gift to you, the reader.

"There is no greater agony than bearing an untold story inside you."
— Maya Angelou, I Know Why the Caged Bird Sings

Over the last year I have had the privilege of reading and editing stories from many women, including those in this book. The joy in my role is hearing them find their voices, using words as the building bricks that give substance to their dreams and desires. Witnessing them stepping into their power. Awakening the goddess within.

Often after many years spent hiding and denying their feelings, their stories, their passions.

Have you got a story burning inside you? Something that you long to share with the world but are too worried or too scared to reveal? Are you longing to release your own divine feminine energy into the world?

Finding your voice, telling your story so far, is an incredibly cathartic experience. Manifesting your divine, feminine magic by setting words in motion is powerful and life changing.

It has irrefutably changed my life.

My childhood involved a great deal of reading. As a shy, slightly reclusive child who spent a great deal of time with grown-ups and learned that it was best to keep quiet to avoid confrontation, I would escape into adventures with the children who populated the stories that I read.

From the sullen, mis-understood Mary who discovered magic in a Secret Garden, to Julian, Dick, Anne, and Georgina (George) – and their dog Timmy, Enid Blyton's The Famous Five. Who went off on amazing adventures with a picnic and a bottle of pop. I escaped into other worlds, my imagination fired by the words of these authors who conjured up worlds of good deeds and excitement.

I identified with Mary, feeling out of place and quite lonely, but oh how I longed to be George. A tomboy, headstrong and courageous, she was not afraid of anything.

I joined these children on their adventures, living in my imagination. A place where the sun always shone, the pop was always fizzy, and I was smart, beautiful, and brave.
"The books transported her into new worlds and introduced her to amazing people who lived exciting lives." – Roald Dahl

In these worlds the children had voices, and were able to articulate their wants, needs and dreams to each other and to adults. When it mattered, they spoke up, always able to find the right words. Whereas I was too scared of saying the wrong thing at the wrong time.

As I grew, I continued to escape reality by burying myself in books, transforming myself into a heroine who everyone would envy and admire and would live happily ever after in a perfect and forgiving world.

Looking back now, somewhat older and wiser, I can see that I carried that fantasy world in my head for a very long time. The disadvantage of that has been that I often found myself lacking. Unable to live up to the image of the heroine that I dreamed of becoming.

I spent most of my life wanting more. Craving some fabulous magical life that always seemed just out of reach. Believing that everyone else was living that way and that I was somehow missing out. Looking for something to believe in.

These desires led to much unhappiness and some very bad decisions. Many years spent in the wilderness of believing that I was not "good enough", that I did not deserve the happiness and security that I longed for. I set out to please people. Putting aside my own needs and desires I allowed and facilitated others to treat me cruelly and accepted their behaviour as something that I deserved.

The agony and pain that this caused seemed to kill something inside me. I felt it shrivel.

But at my core, I knew that with a little nurture it would blossom and grow strong again, propelling me into a real and solid version of that beautiful world that I glimpsed in the books that I still immersed myself in. I had hope.

My capacity for love was immense. I loved well, but not always wisely. My soul vibrated with desire for romance and passion, but time and again I mistook control for those things that I so longed for.

But something happened that changed all that. The day that I held my new-born daughter in my arms. My imaginary world and my reality merged. It would take a while but something inside of me began to stir.

Becoming a mum brings many fears, but it also brings immeasurable courage. Even if you are not able to be brave on your own behalf, you discover a super-power, that allows you fight demons, both real and imaginary, on your child's behalf. Bravery is an interesting thing. Once you feed it, it begins to ferment, until it bubbles up and spills out into the world, unleashing its magic on unsuspecting bystanders! It may wreak some destruction in its wake, but it is a force for good. For me? Well, it released my voice. It allowed me to re-imagine my imaginary life and begin to believe that I could, and should, have it in "real life".

Trapped at the time in a destructive relationship, I felt the first stirrings deep inside me as my goddess began to awake.
She first surfaced online as an alter-ego known as Wench. Her words started to spill out over the ether. Sexy, sassy, divine. Taking no prisoners, knowing that she was entitled to more, that she was worthy and deserving. She drew strength from her audience, and although it was to be a while longer before she would step into her full power, the genie was out of the bottle and there was no stopping her.

Wench remained hidden from my day-to-day life for quite some time. But she was always there, supporting and encouraging me to change the things that were holding me back.

Life is full of practicalities. However big our dreams are we still must pay our bills, put bread on the table and do the things that society demands. So sometimes we continue doing the things we know are limiting us, perhaps even harming us, because that is how we deal with our human life on earth, no matter what our divine mission.

So, for 20 years I went through the motions, still suppressing everything that was bursting to explode out of me. When my world actually exploded, in violence and vitriol, I kept going, dealing with the fall out of debt and fear, clinging to my belief that there was something better out there for us.

It was not all bad, of course. My daughter grew, strong and beautiful, despite some challenges along the way. I met a strong man, who provided love and security for both of us. A man who saw inside of me and was not afraid of what he saw blossoming there. Who nurtured and encouraged me as I started to find my feet.

I began to believe that the life I wanted was available to me, and that I was worthy of it.

Then four years ago I had a seismic shift in my consciousness. A spiritual realisation that brought me home to an understanding about the nature of life. Gave me the faith that I had been looking for all my life.

With that, the veil dropped. And my gorgeous Goddess, previously known as Wench, stepped out into the light and fully into her power. Creativity began to flow, fear dropped away, and I realised that I had been holding on to a whole lot of baggage that I did not need. Physically and mentally. It was time to clear it away.

We changed our lives in many ways. Relocated, I changed career, became a coach to help other women on their journeys, encouraging them to step out and step in. To be unafraid.

Life is peaceful and beautiful, with a gentle symmetry that flows with the nature of the place where we live.

Our home is a faded English Victorian seaside town situated on a massive tidal bay. The ebb and flow of the tides, and the seasons reflected in the hills all around us, contribute to an awareness of the splendour of life and the magic of our existence on this green and blue planet spinning through the cosmos. We are tiny beings but part of something vast and beautiful. It takes my breath away.

I have been a writer for most of my life, although my words were for me alone for a long time. Written in diaries, poetry and short stories never shared. But over time I have begun to share my words. Honestly and revealingly. Without shame or restraint. Speaking my truth.

"You can't get to courage without walking through vulnerability".
 - BRENÉE BROWN

And people started to react and respond. With empathy and gratitude. I got many messages saying "I thought it was only me..."
I began to see that everybody has a story. And I felt sad for all the stories that are left untold. For all the magic that remains locked away or buried.

Let me tell you about my Auntie Rhoda. She was my great aunt, and she was born in Durham, a city in the North East of England, in 1910. She married a widowed Cumbrian man with a baby daughter and raised her and two sons on the edge of Lake Windermere in the Lake District.

She was a redhead, with a wicked tongue and a fierce passion. I spent time with her as a child, and then many years later we reconnected, and I visited her often. She died in 1995 and I miss her. She would love that we have relocated to the area now. When she was in her 80s, we had a conversation about her life, and it was full of longing for what might have been. She was envious of my generation and the choices that women have now, compared to when she was a young woman. She believed we had so much freedom, so many more opportunities. She told me some of her stories, shared some of the dreams that she had as a young woman.

Her life was tinged with regret. But I remember her laughter and her wicked sense of humour, and how well she loved the people she loved. That is her legacy.

There have been many times in the last 25 years when I have thought about that talk with Rhoda. She often comes up in conversation, with my mum, her son and granddaughter, and her friends. She is part of my story.

I have a black and white photograph of her aged 45, in the garden of my grandfather's house. It was my parents wedding day in July 1955. She is dancing, hitching up her dress and there is a glimpse of stocking top. She is surrounded by other family members, all smiling. It is a glimpse of a moment in time, a world full of possibility and laughter.

I feel that we owe it to Rhoda, and other women like her, to take advantage of the freedom that is available to us, and to tell our stories. Out loud, with pride.

I am making it *my* mission to help other women tell their stories. Why should you share your story, and who would want to read it?

This book is being released after a year like no other. Our world has been turned upside down and many of us have had time to reflect on our lives. More than ever before we need and crave **CONNECTION**. What better way to reach out to other people and share your story? Your life may feel ordinary to you, but it might seem extraordinary to someone else. Every story shared is a chance to make someone feel less alone.

Bringing your experiences out of the shadows may reveal that many of the things you think about yourself are not the demons you thought they were. It can be incredibly **HEALING** to shine a light into every corner and share your fears, your hopes, and dreams.

I have four words that are my mantra, my sacred words. Words that I apply to everything I do in life; that have become the core values of my storytelling.

Words that I believe sum up the intention and focus of this wonderful book.

I give them to you. Use them wisely and well.

#Kindness
#Compassion
#Connection
#Love

Penny Thresher - Writers Coach

FREE COACHING, RESOURCES, WORKSHOPS AND NEXT STEPS

We are so committed to supporting your journey into living life Goddesspowered that we have created the **Goddess Academy**!

The academy is FREE and contains a range of supporting resource, training, and opportunities for you to have 121 sessions with some of the co-authors of this book.

To access the free materials, use the link below:
http://bit.ly/joingoddessacademy

You can join our Facebook community:
http://bit.ly/EDGRCommunity

Further reading and listening:

You can find our personal recommendations of books we have all felt inspired by along our own journey -
www.theeverydaygoddessrevolution.com/bookclub

You can listen to some amazing on-demand wellbeing show's and spiritual music at **www.wellbeingradio.co.uk**

If you have any further questions you can contact us via email
Leanne@leannemacdonaldwellbeing.com

THE AUTHORS

Yolandi Boshoff – Soul Coach
www.divinesoul.me

Iona Russell – Intuitive Mindset Coach
www.ionarussell.com

Ceryn Rowntree – Soul Led Therapist
www.cerynrowntree.com

Infiniti Jones – Goddess of healing sound and love
www.themysteriesgone.com/podcast

Wendy Dixon – Spiritual Coach & Psychic Medium
www.wendydixon.co.uk

Judy Prokopiak – Resilience & Spiritual Coach
www.judyprokopiak.com

Scott Hutchison-McDade – Spiritual Teacher
www.positivechangeyoga.com

Lisa Viccars – Holistic Therapist
www.lvholistictheraphy.com

Amy Whistance – Holistic Therapist
www.empowermentcoaching.uk

Randi Willhite – Biofeedback Spiritual Coach
www.wellnessgardenpath.com

Jena Robinson – Energy Healer
www.jenarobinson.com

Shveta S – Intuitive Therapist
www.untetheredgoddess.com

Tierra Womack – Confidence & Wealth Coach
www.thebravewaytribe.com

Karli Kershaw – Inner Work & Relationship Coach
www.karlikershaw.com

Lisa Martin – Curveball Queen
www.thelisamartin.com

Michelle Maslin-Taylor – Holistic Therapist & Yoga Teacher
www.livehappylivehealthy.co.uk

Kimberley Jones – Sacred Feminine Activist
www.healingthewitchwound.co.uk

Tanja Stephanie Rug – Intuitive Coach
www.auxell-coaching.de

Helen Bartram – Happiness Coach
www.helenbartram.com

Trish McKinnley – Spiritual Lifestyle Expert
www.trishmckinnley.com

Jasmin Baljak – Goddess of Wealth Creation
www.facebook.com/jasmin.baljak

Charlie Edwards – Editor & Spiritual Badass
www.untamedsoulmagazine.com

Julie Brown – Women's Empowerment Expert
www.julie-brown.info

Sarah Battle – Spiritual Practitioner & Life Coach
sarahlouisebattle@gmail.com

Penny Thresher – Writers Coach & Editor
www.cornerhousewords.co.uk

www.theeverydaygoddessrevolution.com

Printed in Great Britain
by Amazon

58293528R00108